Come Next Spring

Scripture Reflections of Promise and Hope

D1500867

James R. Welter

Foreword by Rev. Clement T. Davis, Pastor
St. Bartholomew Parish, Columbus, IN

ASCENDING
VIEW
PUBLICATIONS

www.ascendingview.com

The ESV is an "essentially literal" translation which attempts to make the original languages as transparent as possible to the reader. It gives the reader the best view of the original wording of the Biblical writers. The starting point for the ESV was the 1971 Revised Standard Version (RSV). More than 90 percent of the RSV is retained in the ESV. The RSV was regarded by many as the best modern translation in terms of precision and literary elegance.

Layout and Cover Design by Mark A. Welter
Discussion Questions by Helen F. Welter
Edited by James R. Welter II

Cover Photo: early 1900s-era barn – Franklin, IN
Ron Edlin, owner

ISBN: 1-59352-261-4

Printed in the United States of America
by Christian Services Network
El Cajon, CA

Other books by James R. Welter
When Winter Comes - Scripture Reflections for Daily Living
Ascending View Publications, 2003

Dedication

This book is dedicated to My Wife
Helen Ann (Fritz) Welter

In many ways, this has been the most difficult part of the book to write.

I expected it to be easy, to say a few words about the person with whom I have spent most of my life – and it was certainly tempting to borrow a few worn phrases from a romance novel to give testimony to my wife's inspiration and support, which has been essential in bringing this work to life. But to do so would be to trivialize my journey with her; the way has not always been smooth, our path has not always been clear, and our life together has not always been a "given." Nor would it properly acknowledge the dreams that were sacrificed so our relationship might live. Yet, after thirty-seven years, here we are: still together, still hand-in-hand, still companions on that forever journey.

The week before we got married in 1969, my "to do list" seemed endless: I was nervous and stressed, but everything seemed under control until Helen casually asked, "Did you get my ring engraved?"

"Ring engraved?!" I thought. "I'm still a bachelor – how am I supposed to know about these things?"

So I had two days to come up with a phrase that was romantic, poetic, and timeless, and was six words or less! I suddenly got a severe case of "writer's block," and my final choice – "the difference is loving you" – sounded more like an accountant's summary than a lover's ode ... yet the phrase haunted me.

I grew up in the "black-and-white" era of the 1950s. My father, a product of his own European culture, was authoritarian and strict; my mother was passive and expressed little emotion. They were good people and, in their way, I'm sure they loved me... yet I don't recall the words "I love you" ever being spoken in our house. So I grew up without a "felt" sense of being loved.

All of that changed one hot August afternoon, when I was twenty-nine years old and taking Helen home to meet my mother for the first time. Helen was chatting happily about the flatness of the land in northern Indiana and the funny names of the towns we passed through... but I was far away; I was painful *years* away, remembering my sister Fran's advice about our "family secret": "Don't ever tell anyone that our father was in a mental hospital – the school kids will make fun of you and people might think you're crazy too. So don't tell anyone... ever!"

The trip home never seemed so long before... driving Highway 29 and winding through the farmlands of northern Indiana, it just didn't like seem the "short" way home this time. "I need to show you something!" I suddenly blurted out, as I swerved the car on to Highway 25 and drove on to the Logansport State Hospital campus. It was a hot summer day, as I walked with my fiancée to the center of the grounds. It was lunchtime, and the patients were emerging from the buildings by the hundreds from every direction; some of them were talking to themselves, others were clinging to dolls, and many were screaming their pain. With a bewildered look, Helen finally asked, "What *is* this place?" "Look around you," I replied in a stern voice, pointing to a thousand patients – "*this* is my earliest memory; this is my greatest fear. If you have any sense, you'll get in the car and go back to Indianap – ."

I never finished that sentence; instead, I felt her arms around me and I heard her say again and again, "I love you – I love you – I love you." And for the first time in my life, I *felt* loved... and I knew my life would never be the same.

But change did not come easily, and my fears did not go quietly into the night. However, Helen's constant reminders that my love for her and for our sons was but a shadow of God's love for me slowly began to influence my life. And now, finally, I'm coming to know that love drives out fear. That love conquers all. That love sets us free. And, in that freedom, we can dare to let go of societal expectations and self-images... and call forth the gifts and talents long held captive.

At every defining moment of the past thirty-eight years of my life, Helen has encouraged me and supported my decisions, and has always challenged me to even greater heights. Anyone I have touched or influenced in my ministry or with my writing has, in a real way, been touched by Helen too.

So thank you, Helen, for seeing in me what I could not see. For believing that I was more than a mere "provider,"and that I could "be" more than I was "doing". And for letting go of your own dreams, so that I might be whole... and that someday we might truly be one.

"The difference is loving you." Finally, I realized why these words haunted me so – they were yours, written in a poem long ago. And now I can give them back to you in their fullness:

> *Life and happiness fill each hour*
> *And there is warmth*
> *from sunset to dawn.*
> *I ask myself why, what makes it so,*
> *And I hear in the echo*
> *of all that lives*

The difference is loving you!

Foreword

It has become trite to refer to the busy-ness of life; the pace of our lives has steadily increased year after year, and there is no changing that. But what I have found over the past sixteen years is that there are some people who help me to slow down and take notice of my life. They are the members of my Small Church Community– we meet every two or three weeks and, after a reflective reading of the biblical passages scheduled for the coming Sunday and a brief commentary, we use some life-situation questions to open up our minds and hearts. The best questions are taken from our own lives and bring us face-to-face with Christ, who has come to bring us life in abundance! But when we are looking for questions to encourage our reflection and conversation, we also look to other people of faith for ideas.

Jim Welter is such a person of faith. He has wrestled with life's situations and with the Word of God, and he continues to do so. His daily experiences, drawn not only from his rural beginnings but also from his personal relationships in the business world and his life of ministry in the Church, serve him – and his readers – as a lens through which to view the scriptures anew.

I also consider Jim to be something of a pioneer in his use of the Internet to spread the Good News. Over the past six years, the e-mail scripture and reflection ministry he founded at St. Monica Parish has touched the lives of thousands of people around the world. I am delighted that Jim has gathered some of his most thought-provoking reflections into this, his second book, *Come Next Spring – Scripture Reflections of Promise and Hope.*

As you read the reflections in this book, you will be amused by some and saddened by others – but you will always be changed. Jim's memories will help to stir recollections from your own life, and will open windows onto the lush landscape of your relationship with God... so that you, too, may see the promise and hope that He offers.

I invite you to embark on this journey of self-discovery, and to hear God's Word in a new way by reflecting on it in light of Jim's life experience – and your own. You will find that you are indeed "surrounded by a cloud of witnesses" (Heb 12:1) and by no means alone in your faith, nor in your struggles.

Come next spring, you'll be glad that you've taken this spiritual walk with Jim Welter.

In Christ's love,

Fr. Clem Davis

Rev. Clement T. Davis, Pastor
St. Bartholomew Parish, Columbus, IN
Founding Member of the Board,
National Alliance of Parishes Restructuring into Communities

Introduction

"Next Year in Jerusalem!"
(*L'shana ha'ba-ah b'Yerushalayim!*)

Each year at Passover, Jewish people all over the world utter this phrase as they optimistically look forward to leaving their homes and celebrating the next Passover in Jerusalem, fulfilling at last the ancient dream of being a free people in their own land. This particular expression of hope is as ancient and timeless as scripture itself: God's people in exile prayed it a thousand years before the coming of Christ; it has been found etched on prison walls and has been heard chanted in synagogue prayers throughout every nation. For more than two thousand years, "next year in Jerusalem" has been a prayer of hope and a testament to the belief that dreams would ultimately be fulfilled.

In the farm country of Northern Indiana where I grew up, a similar phrase was often used. The words were not as ancient or poetic, but the sense of hope was no less real. I remember our dreams being expressed in the words "come next spring"!

Like the people of scripture, farmers are people of hope – not "hope" defined as "wishful thinking," but hope as an expectation of good. Planting in the spring speaks of hope. A farmer hopes the frosts are gone; he hopes that the sun won't be too hot and that the rains will come at the right times. And if the rains do not come, he lives in expectation... and, in hope, plants his seeds again next year.

I remember a disastrous planting season that occurred when I was about ten years old. The rains had gone on far too long that year, and as I stood in the field with my oldest brother

and the farmer who rented our land, I recall seeing nothing but puddles of water in the soil where cornstalks should have been pushing through the soil. I could feel the mud from that drenched field oozing through the hole in my shoe as we surveyed the failed crop and, knowing this situation meant less food for our family, I started to cry.

Suddenly the farmer's booming voice shattered the silence: "Come next spring," he said, "we'll sow wheat in this field!"

Those are the "ancient words" of hope from my childhood – come next spring!

Come next spring – we'll turn the soil again. Come next spring – new rains will fall. Come next spring – the flowers will bloom and new growth will flourish.

We will live again. We will laugh again. We will love again. Come next spring!

Jesus spoke of hope many times in his parables. The word "parable" comes from the Greek word parabolein, meaning "to throw alongside." In other words, in telling a parable, Jesus is inviting us to place our life experience alongside his stories. The reflections I share in this book, then, are my parables –my life experience placed alongside the passages from scripture. And as you read this book, I invite you to join me on that "parable road" – to place your life experience beside the scripture passages and listen for their meaning in your own life.

The God that we encounter on the parable road can't be contained in the certainties of doctrine, nor limited by our vision, nor controlled by our repeated rituals.

Acknowledgements

My Two Sons:
James R. Welter II, MA, University of Connecticut
Mark A. Welter, BA, Purdue University
Jim, thank you for your countless hours of editing, changing, rewriting, expanding, reworking, clarifying, and otherwise illuminating my thoughts. Almost without exception, you were right – that really *was* "what I meant to say!" I often felt that you took a little too much pleasure in correcting "the old man," but the final revenge is mine – the pride of a father who can say of his son, "He's better at this than I am!"

Mark, thank you for your many creative layout and design ideas, and your assistance in editing. Your contributions make *Come Next Spring* even more appealing and readable, and many will select our book because of the work you have done. And thanks, too, for the design and ongoing maintenance of our website, which makes our book accessible to people all over the world. Your effort helps to put our work in the hands of readers; only then is it possible for us to touch hearts and change lives.

My Wife: Helen A. (Fritz) Welter, RN, CHPN
Thank you for your unfailing and ongoing support, and for contributing the discussion questions. You have the vision and intuition to ask questions that get to the heart of the gospel, and they will be a challenge and a source of spiritual growth for many – as your words have been for me.

Our Infant Grandson: Calvin Joseph Welter
You are what all of us are called to be – "God's love made visible."

The Seven Thousand Subscribers to the St. Monica Parish E-Mail Ministry:
Your affirmation of my scripture reflections and your acceptance of my first book, *When Winter Comes*, have continued to inspire me and to influence my writing.

The First Chapter:
Winter Into Spring

For everything there is a season,
And a time for every matter under heaven:
A time to be born and a time to die;
A time to plant and a time to uproot;
A time to weep, and a time to laugh;
A time to mourn, and a time to dance;
A time to keep, and a time to let go.

(Ecclesiastes 3:1- 6)

I'm not much on "giving things up" for Lent. During my childhood, the season of Lent officially ended at noon on Holy Saturday, and I still have images of standing in the yard with my siblings holding a clock in one hand and a chocolate bar in the other, waiting for the "end of Lent"!

But Lent isn't about endings – it's about beginnings. It's about springtime; it's about turning soil, planting seeds, and experiencing new growth.

Every farmer instinctively knows that soil must first be turned and seeds planted before new life can burst forth. Each farmer knows that something must die to bring forth that new life. And so it is with the winter experiences of our lives: they, too, are a time of preparation – a time for listening, a time for planting, and a time for letting go.

Some of the reflections in this book were very difficult for me to write. I had to walk the fields again and visit places I'd rather not go.

1

That was so easy to write! But now the doctors say my friend's cancer has spread, and nothing more can be done. The treatments have been stopped... and winter has come too soon. Like Mary in this passage, I too want to hold on; I too want things to be the way they were. I want one more vacation together, one more walk on the beach. I want to find one more out-of-the-way restaurant. I want to sit around the pool one more time, and raise one more glass.

Losses remind us how unpredictable, fragile, and precious life is. Loss comes in the midst of living, when our in-box is overflowing and our calendars are full. It's always too soon, and there is always the desire to go back – the desire to hold on to the way things were. We aren't done yet, and it seems that holding on by returning to the way things were will somehow make it easier, or allow us to escape the inevitable.

In our grief, we want to scream "I want my life back!" "I want my youth back!" "I want my health back!" "I want my spouse back!" "I want my friend back!"

Mary came early in the morning, looking for her friend Jesus. At the sound of her name – "Mary" – she reaches out to him. He has come back! Things will again be the way they were! We will walk along the lake, and have quiet talks in the cool breeze of the evening once more. But Jesus says, "Things are no longer the same. For now I must go... and you must let me go."

"Stop holding on to me. Go tell the others, I am going to my Father and your Father."

Tell the others! As long as there is kindness... I live.

As long as there is friendship... I live.

As long as there is love... I live.

And as long as you remember me, as long as you remember our times together... I will be with you.

So be it. Go in peace... dear friend.

In memory of Joan Carr
August 11, 2003

Reflection

1. What person, circumstances or things do you cling to in your life? How can you prepare to "let go"?

2. Why do we want to "hold on" to people, things or circumstances?

3. Do you believe that God is with you in your losses? In what way is God made manifest in these situations?

Come Next Spring

James R. Welter

Listen

Listen, my people, I will speak. **Psalm 50:7**

But you are not to be called rabbi, for you have one teacher, and you are all brothers. And call no man your father on earth, for you have one Father, who is in heaven. Neither be called "Master," for you have one master, the Christ. **Matthew 23:8-10**

I'm not much on "giving things up" for Lent. During my childhood, the season of Lent officially ended at noon on Holy Saturday. I still have images of standing in the yard with my siblings, holding a clock in one hand and a chocolate bar in the other, waiting for the "end of Lent"!

But Lent isn't about endings – it's about new beginnings. It's about springtime; it's about turning soil, planting seeds, and experiencing new growth. Psalm 50 and other scripture passages suggest that Lent is also about listening. Isaiah tells us to "Hear the word of God...listen to the instruction of our God...wash yourselves clean...put away misdeeds...cease doing evil...learn to do good...make justice your aim...redress the wronged...and set things right!" (Is 1:16-20) These are all invitations to action and to relationships. These are invitations to renewal and to a new springtime for our spirit!

The Psalmist echoes God: "Listen, my people, I will speak." And the gospels often tell us that "Jesus spoke to the crowds." These, too, are invitations to hear the Lord – and, by implication, to follow.

The value of "giving something up" for Lent is that it makes us more attuned to listening for the slightest whisper that suggests God is moving in our life and in our relationships.

Identifying the authentic voice of God isn't easy, as Jesus reminds us when he says there is but "one teacher," "one father," and "one master." In our daily life, we are surrounded by many would-be "masters": competing voices, slogans, and ideologies. Lent is a time to discern, identify, and reject the voices of false teachers and to listen for the authentic voice of the "One." It is a time to replace the doldrums of winter with the budding green of spring.

Listen, then, for God's voice as you clear away the "underbrush" that dampens your spirit; listen for God's call as you prune the "branches" of self-confidence or self-doubt. Listen for God's directive in the songs of the returning robins and in the shower of spring rains.

Lent is a forerunner of spring, but we still have much time remaining before the ashes give birth to Easter. We still have an opportunity to live these days well. There is time to stir from the habits of selfish involvement, and time to rip up and re-plant. There is time to listen to our God, who speaks to each of us in our own time and circumstances. Most often, God speaks to us through other people – so, to hear God, we must learn to listen to each other. We must listen deeply to the needs and yearnings of the people in our lives.

To listen for God in each other, we must put aside what we think we "know" and listen deeply for the truth. We must get beyond the mere *appearance* of listening: get beyond taking notes, analyzing the situation, and developing strategies; we must get beyond anything that would put us "in control."

As winter turns into spring, let's simply listen. Let's allow people's needs, yearnings, questions and fears to wash over us like waves upon the shore. Let's just "take it all in."

And somewhere in that wind or in that storm, we will hear God's voice. We will hear God's message. We will hear what we are so often afraid to hear: we will hear our calling.

"Listen, my people, I will speak!"

How will you listen today?

Reflection

1. How and when do you hear God's voice in other people? How has it affected your life?

2. What can you do this Lent to "renew, rip up, and re-plant"?

3. How do you identify the "authentic voice" of God in your life? How will you incorporate that voice when the Lenten season is over?

4. What does "Lent is a forerunner of Spring" mean to you? Why?

I Am Going to Jerusalem   Acts 20:17-22

From Miletus he had the presbyters of the church at Ephesus summoned. When they came to him, he addressed them, "You know how I lived among you the whole time from the day I first came to the province of Asia. I served the Lord with all humility and with the tears and trials that came to me because of the plots of the Jews, and I did not at all shrink from telling you what was for your benefit, or from teaching you in public or in your homes. I earnestly bore witness for both Jews and Greeks to repentance before God and to faith in our Lord Jesus. But now, compelled by the Spirit, I am going to Jerusalem. What will happen to me there I do not know, but you will not see me again."

A few years ago, my wife and I visited Ephesus, which is the setting of this passage from Acts. It's easy for me to imagine the sights, sounds, and smells of that city, and to recreate in my mind what it must have been like when Paul was there. In this passage, Paul is sad and tired, and melancholy permeates his words: "I am going to Jerusalem. I don't know what will happen to me there, but you will not see me again."

Paul does, however, have some idea of what will happen to him in Jerusalem, and Luke makes that clear to us in the ninth chapter of his gospel (Luke 9:51) when he tells us, "Jesus set his face toward Jerusalem." Jesus goes to Jerusalem, where he must face suffering and death. And, in the book of Acts, Luke draws a parallel with Paul's life: Paul's journey will also end in Jerusalem, he too will be arrested and face suffering and death. Then, in the last chapter of his gospel, Luke tells of two disciples on a journey to Emmaus. In that story, one of the disciples is not named. That's Luke's way of

drawing us into the story — *we* are the second disciple! In effect, Luke is saying: "This is what happened to Jesus, and this is what happened to Paul... and, if you choose to walk their path, this is also what may happen to you." For Luke, "going to Jerusalem" is the journey of every Christian.

Paul has mixed emotions about going to Jerusalem; this is a major life change for him, and it's filled with regrets and sadness, anticipation and anxiety. Even now, he feels the dying — the "letting go." There is a yearning to hang on a little longer, to have one more dinner with his friends, to preach to one more crowd, to "run one more race". On the last night that he and his companions were together, they knew that "they would not see him again." They stayed together a little longer that night, and raised their cup a little higher; they hugged a little tighter and told one more story of the good times.

Those same feelings can be sensed as Jesus prepares to "go to Jerusalem" to face his death. "And I am no longer in the world, but they are in the world, and I am coming to you. Holy Father, keep them in your name, which you have given me, that they may be one, even as we are one." (John 17:11)

And so it is with us. We "go to Jerusalem" with each life transition — and each time there is a "letting go." Each time there is a "dying." I lost my job... I'm going to Jerusalem, and part of my identity must die there. My spouse left me... I'm going to Jerusalem, and my relationship must die there. My health is failing... I'm going to Jerusalem, and my self-reliance must die there. I must care for a loved one who is disabled or terminally ill... I'm going to Jerusalem, and much of my freedom must die there.

Easter does not promise an escape from suffering or an exemption from painful life transitions. But Easter does

promise that, on the other side of the transition – on the other side of this "death" – there is new life. And Easter promises that we do not travel alone. Like Jesus, Paul, and the disciples on the road, we develop relationships and form communities that support us, give us strength, and help us grow.

With each life transition and with each step into the unknown, we say with Paul: "I am going to Jerusalem. What will happen to me there I do not know."

Reflection

1. "Going to Jerusalem" is about life transitions. What has been the most difficult transition in your life? Did you know what the outcome would be? Of what did you have to let go as part of this transition? What part of you had to "die"?

2. Recall a time when you were with someone knowing that you "would not see them again"? What was your relationship with that person? What were the circumstances? What was the experience like for you? What did you learn about yourself and your faith?

3. Is there currently a situation in your life that has an unknown outcome? How are you dealing with this uncertainty? What are some things can you do that might be helpful for you during this time?

A Voice in Ramah

Jeremiah 31:15
Matthew 2:18

A voice was heard in Ramah, sobbing and loud lamentation; Rachel weeping for her children, and she refused to comforted, because they are no more.

The news flashed over the airwaves as I began writing this reflection:

"JAKARTA, Indonesia (Dec. 26, 2004) - The world's most powerful earthquake in 40 years triggered massive tidal waves that slammed into villages and seaside resorts across southern and southeast Asia on Sunday, killing more than 7,000 people in six countries."

As the enormity of the tragedy emerged over the days that followed, the final count rose to more than 200,000 people dead. The prophet Jeremiah's cry of agony never seemed more timeless, or more real. That ageless cry reminds us that innocent people still die, whether by the hand of those "who would be king," or as a result of natural disasters. Either way, we are faced with the same questions as the mothers in ancient times, whose sons were killed by the hand of King Herod: "Why them?" "Why now?" Why, O Lord?"

As Christians, how do we explain the crushed homes and flooded streets described in this headline? How do we explain the tragic deaths of innocent people, or why prayers for their rescue seemed to go unanswered? Was there some kind apocalyptic "selection" of those who would live and those who would perish, or were some just in the wrong place at the wrong time? Those who see God as being in control of all things may wonder why one town was destroyed, and not another, or they may see the disaster as some kind of test,

message, or judgment from "on high." Some believers will wonder if their prayers were not answered because their faith was too weak, and some will blame God for allowing – if not causing – such terrible suffering. Others will seek to "defend" God by rationalizing the tragedy, and still others will question the value of prayer or faith.

This is no minor crisis for a believing Christian. Ask someone whose prayers didn't cure cancer or save a loved one from dying, or someone who has led a good and faithful life but now must bury a child. Ask someone who has had to explain a divorce to a tearful young son or daughter, or has lost a job that they loved, or has had a vital relationship fall apart. Deep down, we expect faith to be a transaction: if we believe, then something will happen; if we pray, we will be protected; if we serve, we will be rewarded. And we are distraught to find that this is not always the way things work.

Whether we cling to a script or believe the divine response to be unpredictable and mysterious, we are always unnerved to have our prayers answered by silence... and God's apparent *absence*. We are unnerved by the storm that doesn't pass us by, and we try to explain that which makes no sense to us. Even after our best efforts, some situations simply don't get better, and our attempted explanations seem empty and useless. Sometimes, no matter what we do or say, and no matter how we try to understand or interpret events, the inexplicable reality of the situation just won't go away.

When tragedy strikes, the assurances that religion offers may seem bland and shallow. We often hear things like: "God doesn't give us more than we can handle" (tell that to someone whose family has just drowned in a flood!); "God never closes a door without also opening a window" (I didn't find that very helpful when I lost my job!);

"God must have wanted her more" (what kind of selfish God is that?).

Most of the time, "assurances" like these are of little comfort. Instead, they make us feel bad for doubting, or guilty for wanting to scream in pain, or angry at those who don't seem to understand or appreciate the depth of our suffering.

The truth is that pithy sayings and pious platitudes – the kinds of things I refer to as "bumper-sticker religion" – simply aren't enough to get us through life. Faith needs to be tougher than that; faith needs to be deeper than slogans and cliches, and stronger than ready-made rebuttals. Faith sees the storm and doesn't try to explain it away; faith faces tragedy without having to blame or defend God. Faith believes without proof, lives without answers and assurances, and stands despite suffering and unanswered prayers. And faith knows that, in this world, debits don't always equal credits, the good guys don't always win, and bad things often happen to good people through no fault of their own.

Yet faith doesn't despair. Faith quietly relies on God being there for us, even if we don't see him at work. Faith sees the hurricane coming and says, "If I suffer tonight, Lord, let me see your hand in my neighbor who comes to help. And if I am kept safe, let me be that neighbor to another. Thy will be done." As one song says, faith "believes in God even when he is silent."

Faith isn't about changing the laws of nature – faith is about changing what is in our hearts. Faith is about gaining new sight by turning our attention to those in need; it is about opening ourselves to God's grace and finding the strength to serve. And faith is about experiencing God's love by learning how to love those around us.

14

Faith doesn't explain things; faith accepts what is... and, in all seasons, faith looks for opportunities to love and serve the Lord and his people.

How will you serve him today?

Reflection

1. List some platitudes you have been offered during a difficult time in your life. What was the event and what were the "words of encouragement" or comfort that you were offered? Were these words helpful or comforting to you? Why or why not?

2. What does the phrase "faith sees the storm and doesn't try to explain it away" mean to you? What do you think is the proper role of faith in difficult circumstances?

3. What does our desire to know "why bad things happen to us" say about our faith and our relationship with God? How might we improve this relationship?

Where Was God?   *John 11:17-21*

Now when Jesus came, he found that Lazarus had already been in the tomb four days. Bethany was near Jerusalem, about two miles off, and many of the Jews had come to Martha and Mary to console them concerning their brother. So when Martha heard that Jesus was coming, she went and met him, but Mary remained seated in the house. Martha said to Jesus, "Lord, if you had been here, my brother would not have died."

(Cheryl Welter, my godchild and niece, was killed in an automobile accident three weeks before her eighteenth birthday. This is the reflection I shared at her wake.)

Our gospel tells a story that is all too real for us today: Martha and Mary's brother has died. We don't know much about Lazarus, but we can assume that he was a young man about the same age as Jesus, since they were good friends... and so, we can also assume that his death was an untimely one.

Martha and Mary are in shock and disbelief, just as we are. It's the first stage of the grief that comes with an untimely death. We say things like, "I can't believe it; I just saw him last Monday!" And like us, in a time of tragedy, Martha and Mary send for their friends – including their best friend, Jesus. But for some reason, Jesus delays coming for a few days. Our scripture passage today says, "When Martha heard that Jesus had arrived, she rushed out"! This was the same Martha who had confronted Jesus when her sister wouldn't help in the kitchen, so we can be sure that, when she "rushed out," she was angry and was going to "have it out" with Jesus. "I sent for you three days ago!" she screams. "Why didn't you come?"

16

Then she collapses into her grief: "If you had been here, Lord, my brother would not have died!"

Martha has the same questions that we have tonight: why my daughter? Why my sister? Why my friend? Why Cheryl? Why now? She was so young! We too want to scream, "If you had been here, Lord, Cheryl would not have died!"

Why? You have a right to ask that question. You have a right to be angry: your daughter, your sister, your granddaughter, your friend is gone. Taken away without warning, in a freak accident. You didn't even get a chance to say good-bye to her. It's not fair! You just want to shake God and say, "Where were you?" And this gospel passage tells us that it's OK to feel that way.

Martha screams for all of us today: *why?* Harold, Becky, Nathan, Susan, Laura... I can't answer that question for you tonight. None of us can. All I can tell you is what I believe. I can't speak to everyone's faith; others may look at it differently. But maybe, by sharing what I believe, I can help you to work through some of your own pain.

Let me tell you first what I *don't* believe about God:

I don't believe that this tragedy happened to teach us a lesson; God doesn't parlay one life against another. God isn't going to cause a person to die to teach me something – that would imply that my life is more important than someone else's... and love doesn't work that way.

I don't believe that God caused this tragedy at all. It's our human condition: we don't live in the perfect world God created; we live in a world that reflects the choices of human beings. And sometimes those are not even bad

17

choices; sometimes they are good choices! A young person is in a hurry to get home to her family – there's nothing wrong with that!

I don't believe that God deals the cards. Fate deals the cards; our human condition deals the cards. Oh, we like to *think* God does... somehow it seems that, if God dealt the cards, we would get a fair hand. If we lived right, if we did the things we're supposed to do; if we loved enough, or had enough faith... then nothing bad would happen to us. But nowhere in scripture are we promised that! What scripture does promise is that God will be with us. Scripture does promise that God will care for us, and that good will come out of the bad things that sometimes happen to us.

Now let me tell you what I *do* believe about God:

I believe that God can bring good out of suffering. God doesn't cause suffering, God redeems it – God brings good out of it. How many parents have hugged their children a little tighter today, because of Cheryl? How many times in the last few days has someone said "I love you" to someone they care about, because of Cheryl?

There is one final thing that I believe about God, which I want to share with you. This I believe more than anything else: God is with us; God feels our pain. This may be hard to understand, given the nature of God. How can *God* feel pain? Isn't God perfectly happy in heaven? I can't explain that either. But we know the nature of love, and we know that, when someone we love suffers... we feel the pain. So God, who is love, must somehow feel our pain. And the closing words in this gospel story tell us that. These words comprise the shortest verse in scripture: "Jesus wept." Listen to that verse: it says "God cried"!

Cheryl was a regular kid: she loved to dance, she played in the band, and she was a terror on the tennis court. She harassed her brother and was never convinced that it was her turn to do the dishes. Like most teens, she didn't think she should have to work for her allowance. What Cheryl really liked was to drive the car, and she would make up any excuse to do it. "Hey, Mom – do you need anything from the drugstore? I'll go get it for you!" "Dad, why don't I drive to school? Then you won't have to come and get me." And to her friends, "Need a ride? I'll stop by and pick you up after the game, and take you home."

Where was God? You have a right to ask that question. God said he would be with us... so where *was* God? We want to scream, "Where was God on Thursday night? Where was God when my daughter died?"

I'll tell you where God was that night: God was busy. God was stopping by on Highway 35, just north of town... to pick up Cheryl Welter... and take her home.

Reflection

1. Do you believe that God "deals the cards" of life, and/or has a plan for your life and directs events? If so, how do you reconcile your understanding of "God's plan" with the notion of human free will? With the notion of fate? Of probability, chance, or luck? Is it even possible to reconcile these ideas?

2. Why do you think tragedies, like the untimely death of a young person, occur? What do you believe God's role is in such matters? Could God prevent these tragedies if he chose? If so, why doesn't he do so? Do you think it's even possible to know the answers to these questions? Why or why not?

3. What do and don't you believe about God? List three things that you believe about God, and three things that you do not believe about God. What led you to these conclusions about God?

4. Are any of your answers in question two or three at odds with the confession of your formal faith community? In what ways? And how do you view those differences? Are they reconcilable? Why or why not?

5. What event has happened in your life that has caused you to doubt or to feel that God was not actively present? Why do you feel that way? Has time, prayer, or experience since that event caused you to feel differently?

A Grain of Wheat   John 12:24

Truly, truly, I say to you, unless a grain of wheat falls to the ground and dies, it remains a grain of wheat; but if it dies, it bears much fruit.

My wife Helen was obviously upset at dinner one evening, so I tried to ask a question that would acknowledge her concerns and encourage her to express her feelings. "Did you lose a patient today, dear?" I asked, in my most understanding voice. "I'm a good nurse," was her terse reply. "I don't 'lose' patients – I know where all of them are! But I did have a patient who *died* today."

Without realizing it, I had been using one of those artificial, death-denying terms that are so prevalent in our society. No one "dies" in our all-too-polite world; we "lose" them, they "pass away" or "go to heaven"! In macho terms, they get "wasted," "whacked," "blown away," or become "casualties." We are so uncomfortable with death that we can't even bring ourselves to say the word, and society reinforces our illusions. Commercials whisper to us, "You can stay young forever if you eat our food, join our spa, take our medicine, or use our product!" They imply that aging isn't normal, and that death doesn't have to come. And society whispers to us, "Your value is in your possessions; you are what you have, you deserve it, and nobody else can take it from you!" And we believe these lies, and put our security in material things. We live in the illusion that death can be put off forever. And the pumping of a respirator and the drip of an IV tell us it is so!

Yet Jesus reminds us that everything must die! And he tells us that this is a good thing... that it's necessary for our growth. Still, we fight against the darkness, rather than surrender to the light!

Henri Nouwen speaks of "living with open hands." He reminds us that we are born with our fists clenched, as if shouting, "I!" "Me!" "Mine!" But, he says, we all die with our hands open. Christian life, then, is about learning to let go, learning to live with "open hands."

The gospels, similarly, remind us that we are merely stewards of the earth; they remind us that we don't own the vineyard! Everything we have and everyone we love is "on loan" from God – we get to use those possessions and love those people, but sooner or later they must go back to the One who gave them to us. At which point we can try to hold on to them, kicking and screaming, as they are pried from our clenched fists... or we can graciously, lovingly, and freely let them pass from our lives.

We can fight against the darkness – or we can surrender to the light!

Even so, like the last leaf that clings to the tree in winter, we deny death. We deny death anytime we experience a loss and refuse to let go and move on; we try to deny death when we become prisoners of our past and continue to live out of our loss. Like that last leaf of winter, we can't live in our dead past and also grow. We can't "be" in two places at once: we can't cling to the past *and* live in the present; we can't cling to our fears *and* trust in God. We can't harbor resentment *and* be forgiven; we can't be selfish *and* love freely... and we can't try to have everything our way *and* be open to the movement of the Spirit.

For our continued life and growth, something in us must always fall to the ground and die.

What must you let fall to the ground today?

Reflection

1. Are you clinging to something in the past that prevents you from fully participating in the present?

2. What must you let "fall to the ground" today so that you can grow in your relationship with God?

3. The ultimate "letting go" is death. How can you prepare for it?

Why Do Bad Things Happen?   Job 1:20-21

*Then Job arose and tore his robe and shaved his head
and fell on the ground and worshiped. And he said,
"Naked I came from my mother's womb, and naked
shall I return. The LORD gave, and the LORD has
taken away; blessed be the name of the LORD."*

Our youngest son Mark is an avid reader of novels, but he
won't attend any movie that's based on a book he has read.
"They always insist on a 'Hollywood ending'," he laments,
"and it usually misses the point of the author's work!"

There are many examples in scripture in which later writers
have added a "Hollywood ending" or otherwise modified a
story. The multiple endings of Mark's gospel provide
indisputable evidence of the kind of "story revisions" that
would be familiar to any movie scriptwriter. These changes
in how scripture stories are told often reflect a change in
audience from that of the original setting, or a difference in
the problems or situations that were being addressed.
Sometimes, however, it seems that later editors or writers
just didn't understand the style of the original author, or the
original ending didn't serve their purpose – so, like Hollywood
script editors, they simply (for good or ill) changed it to suit
themselves.

There are many passages in both Christian and Hebrew
scriptures that deal with the timeless question of "why people
suffer." The ninth chapter of John's gospel opens with such a
question: "And his disciples asked him, 'Rabbi, who sinned,
this man or his parents, that he was born blind?'" (Jn 9:1-2)
Paul talks about suffering in his first letter to the Corinthians,
but falls short of answering the "why" question – he simply
tells us that our suffering has meaning. According to Paul,

suffering is meant to bind us all together in a human community: "If one member suffers, all suffer together..." On the other hand, he says, everyone in the community also shares in the rejoicing: "...if one member is honored, all rejoice together." (1Cor 12:26).

Similarly, Matthew also talks about suffering but doesn't answer the "why" question. In his version of the beatitudes, Matthew challenges us to "just hold on," because better times are on the way. If you are in pain now, he says, hold on – for "you will inherit the Kingdom of Heaven." And he reminds us that God will ultimately reward us for our suffering: "Blessed are you when others revile you and persecute you and utter all kinds of evil against you falsely on my account. Rejoice and be glad, for your reward is great in heaven" (Matt 5:11-12).

But, even as a teenager, our philosopher-son Jim would never let Matthew's position go unchallenged! "So God allows us to suffer, just so he can reward us later? I have some problems with that..." (This kid was a teenager for a long, *long* time!) As an accountant, I always liked it when he numbered his arguments: "...(1) That doesn't say much for God, for God to torture us so cruelly and sadistically... and (2) even if you accept that God allows us to suffer so he can reward us later, that still doesn't explain why suffering exists in the first place! Does God cause it? If so, how can he be a loving God? And can he prevent it? If he can't, then how can he be all-powerful? And if he can but won't, how can he truly care about humanity?" (When he was younger, I would send him to his room for arguing like that!)

The Book of Job is the Hebrew scriptures' classic attempt to address the question "Why Do Bad Things Happen to Good People?" – which was how the problem was phrased

twenty years ago by Rabbi Harold Kushner, in his best-selling book of the same name.

In the wisdom literature of the Hebrew Scriptures (that is, the Biblical books of Genesis, Deuteronomy, Job, and the prophets), the Lord is portrayed as a just God who favors those who obey him and punishes those who do not. The story of Job, however, is the tale of a man who obeys God perfectly and yet suffers profoundly. And Job, in his suffering, asks that timeless question for all of us: *why?*

Why did my marriage end in divorce? Why did my loved one die? Why did I lose my job? Why do I have this debilitating disease? Why can't I heal this relationship? Why did 9/11 happen? Why do we have hurricanes, earthquakes, and natural disasters? Why? Why? *Why?*

In the story, Job was a good person – he had done nothing wrong! He was devoted to God and to his loved ones. And when everything was taken from Job – including his livestock, his family, his property, and even his health – Job did not raise his voice in complaint against God. As the story goes on, we see Job's friends attempting to explain his plight through the traditional religious view of divine retribution: as punishment for something Job has done wrong. For Job's friends, the workings of divine providence must be precise and mathematical; everything must make sense and fit together. And in our own day, we like it that way too! When we see someone suffering, we want to fix it, or at least be able to explain it. We want their suffering to end, and we want to put an end to our unanswered questions – and the anxiety and discomfort they cause us. There is a feeling that, if we could understand the "why" of the person's suffering, we would know how to stop it – or if not, at least we could understand it, and this would somehow make the pain easier to bear.

But even when Job's friends came to console him and suggest that he is being punished for some unknown sin, Job's integrity prevails and he still praises God: "The Lord gave and the Lord has taken away; blessed be the name of the Lord!" (Job 1:21).

When it is God's turn to redress the common explanations for Job's plight, God pointedly reminds Job that God is God, while Job is a creature made by him, and that Job should not presume to understand God's ways. Period. Even when Job repents, covered in dust and ashes, he is still seated atop a dunghill in total devastation. And this is the original ending of the story: Job is pondering God's mysterious ways while sitting on a pile of manure! The "Hollywood ending," which tells of Job's complete restoration, was a later addition to the text – and completely misses the point. (Evidently the original ending was too grim for even some scripture writers to accept!)

Unfortunately, however, the original "Job" explanation for suffering – which is *no* explanation at all! – is the only one we have. Job's original text leaves us with the idea that suffering is simply an inexplicable mystery of life.

Anyone who has ever watched the innocent suffer, however, must conclude that suffering cannot come from a loving God, and that God does not desire it for us. Scripture tells us that God desires our good and loves us unconditionally! And surely this would seem to preclude God's putting us through suffering and pain just so he can reward us for good behavior in the next life.

But the bottom line is that, as the story of Job tells us, we cannot know the answer to why we suffer, nor can we comprehend God's role or purpose in such events. Like Job, we cannot understand God's unfathomable ways – we can

only hold on to our faith in him, as Job did, come what may. Perhaps God has some greater good in store, or some larger purpose that we cannot yet perceive. Perhaps one day we will know the answer... or perhaps we never will. But in any case, we do know *this* much: that suffering is a fundamental part of life and not a sign of God's abandonment. Even in the original version of the story, although he doesn't explain himself, God never abandons Job. And the gospels show us that suffering is a condition God willingly shares with us in the person of Jesus.

Like Job, I don't have the answer to why suffering exists. I don't know why bad things happen to good people, nor why God doesn't spare them – no one knows that. Even Jesus prayed for the cup of suffering to be taken from him, but it was not.

However, like the apostle Paul, I believe that suffering does have meaning. I believe it binds us to each other and to God. And perhaps this is its larger purpose: in that binding, in that sharing – in that "holding on" together – and in the sympathy, compassion, and love that is born from it...

...we will come to inherit the kingdom.

Reflection

1. Why do you think suffering exists? Why do you think God allows people to suffer, especially the innocent? Why doesn't he prevent it? Do you think we can ever know the answers to these questions? Why or why not?

2. Do you think there is purpose in suffering? If so, what is the purpose?

3. If God offered to answer one question about your life, what would you ask him to explain to you? What do you think his answer to your question might be? What helps you to go on without knowing God's answer?

4. There is an ancient Eastern prayer which asks: "Grant me appropriate trials and suffering... so that my practice of detachment from worldly concerns and universal compassion may be fulfilled." What does this prayer imply about the purpose or meaning of suffering? Do you think you could ever say this prayer with conviction? Why or why not?

Come Next Spring
James R. Welter

It Was Night
John 13:21-38

"Amen, amen, I say to you, one of you will betray me." Judas took the morsel and left at once. And it was night.

When I returned to college a few years ago as a "non-traditional student," my favorite class was creative writing. Often, the assignment was to read a piece of literature, reflect on our experience of it, and then dissect the writing to determine how the author was able to "get us into" that time or place. For me, it was frequently the author's use of short, blunt sentences of seemingly gratuitous information that created the feeling of "being there." Hemingway was a master of this technique, with his one-word sentences: "1942." "Rain." "Dark." I think the writer of today's gospel was also familiar with this technique. "And it was night." Somehow, I don't think he was just telling us the time of day!

Our cosmopolitan lifestyles and the restlessness of our lives tend to blur the line between day and night. But in ancient times, before the invention of electric lighting, darkness was all but impenetrable and night was a time when evil spirits roamed the land and enemies approached in stealth. The creation story in Genesis reflects this idea: God created light and "saw that it was good." "Then God separated the light from the darkness." (Genesis 1:3-4)

"Get home before dark" isn't an admonition given to young people very much these days, but it was a common one when I was growing up on the farm. With the exception of an occasional barnyard pole lamp, the "outside lights" were the moon and the stars, and a walk home on a cloudy night could be treacherous. Back then (and even more so in Biblical times), the contrast between day and night was a stark one, and it was representative of a similar thought process

30

of polar opposites: Jew or Gentile, slave or free, male or female, Protestant or Catholic, mortal or venial, good or evil, right or wrong, "them" or "us." The instances of "gray" were few.

And into this world of stark contrasts comes Jesus, who is "grayness" personified! Jesus blurred many comfortable distinctions: he walked freely onto Gentile soil, embraced women and men equally, spoke of compassion toward enemies, refused to answer yes-or-no questions, and saw the nuances of apparently simple matters like observance of the Sabbath, traditional doctrines, and customary rituals.

It was night!

Even today, we still love stark contrasts, especially in times of uncertainty. We love the simplicity of "black and white" distinctions, which allow us to label and mentally assert control over matters: red-state or blue-state, conservative or liberal, Catholic or Protestant, saved or unsaved, pro-war or anti-war, "with us" or "against us." Among many there is a profound distrust of nuance, diversity, ambiguity, tolerance, or any blurring of sharp boundaries. That distrust often claims to be holy, biblical, righteous, or Christian – but most often it simply reflects fear.

It was night!

Jesus proclaims that "one of you will betray me" – and we must *all* leave the room, or else stand with Peter and futilely deny our own dark side. Like Judas, we betray our master whenever we refuse to accept Jesus as he is, with his ever-present challenge to our status quo. We betray our master when we don't love enough, forgive enough, or accept others where they are – or for whom they are. We betray our master

when we try to manipulate God or somehow compel God to do our bidding. We betray our master whenever we let fear control our lives, or allow it to prevent us from loving our neighbor.

It was night!

The "Judas" in me screams for God to change, to do things differently... to do it *my* way! But God will not change. Rather, he wants *me* to be changed.

Have you let Jesus come into *your* world of stark contrasts? Have you changed a "traitorous" belief, attitude, habit, judgment, or behavior this Lenten season? Have you allowed the light of Christ to shine more brightly in your heart, and in your life?

Or is it still night?

Reflection

1. What fears in your life causes you to betray your Master?

2. How might you turn your fear into faith?

3. What "stark contrasts" do you see in your world? How do they affect your life?

4. Who or what helps you allow Christ to shine more brightly in your life?

Choose Life   Deuteronomy 30:19

See, I have set before you this day life and death, good and evil... therefore choose life.

I didn't know him personally, but he often read at Sunday Mass. His towering presence, deep voice, and studied diction were surely the envy of every Baptist preacher. I was only at his funeral to lend community support to the family. Instead of a eulogy, the oldest son read a letter that his father had written in his final days. A hush fell over the congregation; there was a sense that we were in a sacred place, on holy ground. It was like being at a deathbed. We knew that the words that were read would reveal this man's very soul.

Deathbed moments are rare in a society like ours, in which eighty percent of people die in institutions such as hospitals or nursing homes. But it has not always been so: history and literature record powerful moments of dying. And those final moments – the last words – are often used to teach, instruct, and summarize one's life. A whole literary genre, in fact, has developed around these sacred moments. Examples can be found throughout the whole of Greco-Roman literature (partly inspired by Socrates' farewell to his disciples in Plato's *Phaedo*). This genre has a defined format: the patriarch, hero, or master, is about to die and gathers his children, followers, disciples, or students around him and offers lessons from his life, as well as warnings, curses, blessings, instructions, and hopes for their future. Finally, he dies and is laid to rest, having entrusted his most important gifts to his followers.

Moses' farewell speech in this passage from Deuteronomy is an example of this genre as it appears in the Hebrew scriptures. And we have examples in the New Testament as well, as Jesus gives final instructions to his disciples,

33

telling them, "Take up your cross daily and follow me." We tend to listen attentively to the final words of those we follow or admire, because those words often reveal what was most important in their lives. Moses says, "I have set before you life and death, the blessing and the curse. Choose life." And Jesus says, "For whoever wishes to save his life will lose it, but whoever loses his life for my sake will save it." "Choose life" is the hope and final instruction of both Moses and Jesus. It is their legacy to us.

So, how are we to choose life? Jesus is specific: "Deny yourself, take up our cross daily, and follow me."

Being a Christian is a lifelong journey to the center of our very self. It is only there that we can see what we must deny ourselves. It is only there that we can see what we must let go of... if we are to *choose life*. It is not by accident that the liturgical season of Lent ends in the spring. The new life of spring can only come forth if something else dies. Lent is not primarily a "penitential season" – it's a growing season! It requires us to determine what we must "allow to die" in our own lives. Then we will know what must be done in order for us to become "a new creation."

Christian life must not be merely a series of behaviors performed by rote; rather, it must be a life lived out of the questions we ask. These questions are posed to measure our progress – our growth – on the way to the fullness of life.

In scripture, we hear the last words of Jesus and we know we are in a sacred place; we are on holy ground. We hear his instructions.

Do we dare to ask the question: "Master, what must I do to choose eternal life?"

Reflection

1. Have you ever been present when someone died? What was the experience like? Did you hear the person's last words? What impact did those words have on you?

2. What does the author mean by the phrase, "Being a Christian is a lifelong journey to the center of our self"?

3. What do you want your death to be like? Would you want to know that you are dying? What would your last words be?

4. Salvation is a free gift from God, but we must choose to accept or reject that gift. What would your answer be to the question, "Master, what must I do to choose eternal life"?

I Have Seen the Lord   Luke 24:1-3, 9-11

But on the first day of the week, at early dawn, they went to the tomb, taking the spices they had prepared. And they found the stone rolled away from the tomb, but when they went in they did not find the body of the Lord Jesus. And returning from the tomb they told all these things to the eleven and to all the rest. Now it was Mary Magdalene and Joanna and Mary the mother of James and the other women with them who told these things to the apostles, but these words seemed to them an idle tale, and they did not believe them.

The glow of a streetlight outlines the shadow of a man searching the ground. A passing stranger stops and asks him, "What are you looking for?" "I lost my house key," the searching man replies. "How did you lose your house key in the street?" the stranger asks. "I didn't lose it in the street," says the man, "I lost it in the house." "Well, if you lost your key in the house," asks the surprised stranger, "why are you looking for it out here in the street?" And the man answers, "Because the light is better out here!"

In the scripture passage above, Mary Magdalene rushes back to the apostles and breathlessly reports that she has "seen the Lord." But the apostles thought the story "seemed like nonsense" and didn't believe her. It is clear from the gospels that Mary has a close relationship with Jesus; it is from her that he is said to have cast out seven demons, and Mary is always listed first when the female disciples are mentioned. She is at the foot of the cross when Jesus dies, and it is to her that Jesus first appears after his resurrection. Yet the apostles do not believe that she "has seen the Lord." They do not believe her because they are blinded by their own expectations, experiences, and preconceptions. They operate

from what they think they "know" – and they "know" that no one can rise from the dead! They "know" that, if Jesus *did* appear, it would first be to a man! (In the patriarchal culture of their time, a woman couldn't be a legal witness because female testimony wasn't considered reliable.) The apostles can't see the truth because they are looking "in the street, where the light is better"! They limit their "search" to areas in which they feel comfortable; they stick to what they "know." And they fail to believe the truth.

But Mary understands. When she went to anoint the body of Jesus that morning, she made the same mistake. She, too, looked in the wrong place. She looked "where the light was better" – in a place where it would be easy to see him. She looked where she *expected* to find him, where he was "supposed to be." She looked in the tomb.

We, too, look "where the light is better" – we look where we are comfortable, we look through the filters of our perceptions, experience, expectations, and prejudices. We look in the tomb. Yet, if we are to see Jesus and recognize him in our lives, we too must "come out of the tomb." We must come out of the "tomb" of our painful past, of our destructive relationships and binding habits, of our past hurts and disappointments. We must come out of the "tomb" of doctrines that rigidly define God, or beliefs that limit where we may see him. To see Jesus, we must be willing to let go of all we "know"; we must leave the comfortable light of the streetlamp and peer into the darkness of our own "house." For it is there that all searches must ultimately lead us, because "the kingdom of God is within you." (Luke 17:21)

The tomb is empty.

He lives in you!

Reflection

1. Most of us tend to live our lives "where the light is better" – in other words, we stay in our "comfort zone." Consider your "comfort zone." What are its parameters and restrictions? (Some may be personal habits, set schedules, patterns of thought, etc.) What are some things that you claim you will "never do"? What goals or desires of yours remain unfulfilled because the experience would be outside your comfort zone? How does your comfort zone limit your freedom? How does it limit your ability to live the gospel message?

2. When was a time when you were "blinded" by your own expectations or preconceived ideas? What can you do to help prevent such "blindness" in the future?

3. Like Mary, we sometimes do not recognize Jesus because he appears in an unlikely place (like walking in a garden when he's supposed to be dead!). Where is Jesus least likely to be found in your life and world? How can you begin to look for him there?

4. The life of Jesus invites us – even *compels* us – to leave our comfort zone. Resolve to do one thing that takes you outside your comfort zone. Asking yourself the liberating question "what will happen if I _____?" may help you to take that step.

5. What was the experience in question four like for you?

Show Us The Father **John 14:8-10**

Philip said to him, "Lord, show us the Father, and it is enough for us." Jesus said to him, "Have I been with you so long, and you still do not know me, Philip? Whoever has seen me has seen the Father. How can you say, 'Show us the Father'? Do you not believe that I am in the Father and the Father is in me?

When the final homilies have all been spoken this Easter season, and we have reflected on the significance of the death and resurrection of Jesus, and the final words for this holiday have been penned... the Easter message will be no more eloquently spoken nor profoundly stated then in the words of a children's song: "Jesus came to show us what God is like."

Many Christians seem to have a pretty poor image of God. We often attribute deeds of revenge and destruction to God that we wouldn't otherwise blame on our worst enemy. When we experience floods, airplane crashes, or natural disasters – all too often, it seems that God ends up being the "bad guy." Maybe this poor image of God results from our negative relationship with our own father, or from societal perceptions of what fatherhood is all about. Maybe it results from faulty theology. Perhaps it comes from how we interpret scripture. Whatever the root cause, many Christians have an image of God that is simply not consistent with the loving Father that Jesus revealed to us. When we think of Jesus, we usually imagine a warm, kind, and merciful person. But when we think of his Father, we often imagine an old man with a long white beard, who sits in stern judgment of our actions.

Those of us who were raised in the Baltimore Catechism era of Catholic teaching came by our poor image of God

quite honestly. In that era of black-and-white indoctrination, we experienced a legalistic God — an all-knowing policeman in the sky... an accountant God who kept track of our lives in columns of right and wrong... a grim "Santa Claus" God, who made a list and checked it twice!

And yet, this problem with our image of God is not a new one. The apostles themselves had the same problem!

During his public ministry, Jesus spoke many times of his Father, and of his Father's love for us — yet one day, Philip says to Jesus, "Lord, show us the Father." And Jesus gets a little upset, and he replies: "For a long time I have been with you all; yet you do not know me, Philip. Whoever has seen me has seen the Father. Why, then do you say, 'Show us the Father'? Do you not believe, Philip, that I am in the Father and the Father is in me?"

A literal reading of the Old Testament may leave us with the image of an intolerant, judgmental God, who strikes down all those who oppose him. Yet, if we read those texts in their fullness, we see a picture emerging over time of a faithful God, a loving Father who is always there for us. And we see the scripture writers, in both the Old and New Testaments, growing in their understanding of God until, at last, John can write: "God is Love." (1John 4:8)

Notice that John doesn't say "God *shows* love"; he doesn't say "God *has* love" — he says God *is* love! In other words, it is the very nature of God to love. And if this is so, then God doesn't kill people. God doesn't cause sickness, crash airplanes, or bring about natural disasters. And God doesn't keep score. He simply loves!

I think of God's love as being like the sunshine. The very nature of the sun is to shine! Now, I can go into my house, close the drapes, and separate myself from the warmth and light of the sun... but the sun will continue to shine! And so it is with God's love: I can drape myself in selfishness and separate myself from God, but God continues to love. And, at my option, I can step into his light and feel the warmth of his Son.

If our image of God the Father is different from our image of Jesus his Son... then we are like Philip – we don't know the Father! And we don't really understand Jesus, either.

Throughout his entire public ministry – by forgiving sinners, healing the sick, accepting the outcast – through countless words and deeds of love and mercy – Jesus tried to reveal his Father. In the words of that children's song, Jesus tried to "show us what God is like." But, like us, Philip had so many negative, false images of God that when Jesus spoke of God as a loving Father, Philip couldn't reconcile that image with the God that he "knew"! So he says, "Lord, show us the Father!" Show us this loving Father you're talking about.

We can almost hear the frustration in Jesus' voice as he replies, "Philip, how can you say 'Show us the Father'?" Have you not seen *me* all this time? How else *can* I show you the Father? How else can I show you what God is like? How can I make you understand the depth of the Father's love?

Anyone who has been a teacher, even on a limited basis, has experienced a similar frustration: the frustration of trying to convey an idea that is beyond the student's ability to grasp or understand. We often encounter the same difficulty in dealing with our own children. Have you ever tried to tell your teenager how much you love him or her? We parents

41

usually end up by saying something like, "Wait until you have children of your own – then you'll understand!" Or have you ever asked a small child to express his love for you? Have you ever asked something like, "How much do you love Mommy?" or "How much do you love Daddy?" The child, unable to express himself, finally throws out his arms and says, "See? I love you *t-h-i-s* much!"

One day, Jesus finally found a way to express the Father's love to Philip – and to us.

With his arms outstretched on the cross, he seems to be saying: "See... I love you... this much."

Reflection

1. What is your image of God as Father? Is it a positive image, or a negative one? Why?

2. When you pray, to whom do you address your prayers? To God? To Jesus? To a Saint? Why?

3. What image of God did you hold as a child or teenager? How has your image of God changed over the years? What cause this image to change?

4. And old Eastern saying goes: "To see God, we must first remove the mask we have placed on him." What does this mean? How can we go about removing God's "mask"?

Look Beyond   *John 6:30-35*

So they said to him, "Then what sign do you do, that we may see and believe you? What work do you perform? Our fathers ate the manna in the wilderness; as it is written, 'He gave them bread from heaven to eat.'" Jesus then said to them, "Truly, truly, I say to you, it was not Moses who gave you the bread from heaven, but my Father gives you the true bread from heaven. For the bread of God is he who comes down from heaven and gives life to the world." They said to him, "Sir, give us this bread always." Jesus said to them, "I am the bread of life; whoever comes to me shall not hunger, and whoever believes in me shall never thirst."

The chosen people had always regarded the manna in the wilderness as the "bread of God" (Psalm 78:24, Exodus 16:15). There was a strong belief that, when the Messiah came, he would duplicate Moses' feat and also provide manna from heaven. So, in the above passage, the people are asking Jesus to produce manna from heaven as proof of his claim to be the Messiah. But Jesus responds by telling them that the manna Moses gave was not the true "bread from heaven," but only a symbol of the "bread" which was to come and which would give life to the world. And he challenges them to look beyond tradition when he tells them, "*I* am the bread of life."

Back in the pre-Vatican days, we Catholics put a lot of emphasis on the objects or "elements" of the Eucharist – that is, the physical bread and wine. We memorized the doctrine of "transubstantiation" (which was the church's official definition of how Jesus was present in the Eucharist) and we argued about exactly when the "consecration" actually took place. But in scripture, we see that emphasis isn't placed so much upon the elements as it is upon the *action*:

"They recognized him in the *breaking* of the bread."
(Acts 2:42)

We, too, are challenged to look beyond the "manna" – to look beyond the elements that are present when we celebrate the Eucharist. In the words of the hymn: "Look beyond the bread you eat / see your Savior and your Lord / Look beyond the wine you drink / see his love poured out as blood."

To truly experience Jesus, we must look beyond literal definitions and rigid dogma. The discussion about the "real presence" and what it means isn't an argument to be won – it is a path to be followed, a life to be lived. The *question* is what challenges us and defines us: how am *I* "real" to those around me? How am *I* "present" to those in need? How am *I* the "real presence" of Jesus in the world?

We must look beyond the objects: the Eucharist isn't a "thing," it's an *action* – it is something we *do*. And the "elements" aren't merely what we are to eat, they're what we are to *become*... bread broken and wine poured out. In the final analysis, it isn't bread and wine that Jesus wants to transform – it's *us*.

Look beyond the bread you eat: see his body broken, and freely given... for you.

Look beyond the wine you drink: see his life poured out; see how he emptied himself... for you.

Lord! Let *me* be broken and given; let me be crushed and transformed.

Let me be a sign... that they might believe in you!

Reflection

1. Have you ever asked God for a "sign" as an answer to a prayer? What was the result? What does that result – and the request you made – reveal about you or your faith?

2. How do you understand or explain the "real presence" of Christ in the Eucharist? How does thinking of yourself as *becoming* part of that "real presence" change your understanding of the Eucharist?

3. Do you think this emphasis on *becoming* part of Christ's "real presence" through the Eucharist would be acceptable to most Christians? Why or why not?

4. Do you believe that Christians must be of one mind in their understanding of the Eucharist, in order to invite each other to a common sharing of communion? Why or why not?

The Second Chapter:
Flowers Bloom

Lo, the winter is past
the rain is over and gone
flowers appear on the earth.
                    (Song of Solomon 2:11-12)

"I heard a tractor this morning."

Mom's breakfast comment echoed one of the first signs of spring on the farm. The sound of a tractor meant that we had survived another winter, and that things would now be better... at least for a while. Soon, the orchard would be alive with the scent of apple blossoms, and their fruit would burst forth and be ours for the taking. Mulberries on the tree would be a precursor of blackberries on the vine, and spring rains would cause the mushrooms to sprout.

"I heard a tractor this morning."

It was the sound of soil being turned and seeds being planted; it was the sound of hope being renewed and life beginning once again. In the springtime, flowers bloom, and in the early sun, Morning Glories turn toward the light and bow to our renewed hope.

I heard a tractor this morning...

...it's time to begin anew.

Look At the Birds   Matthew 6:26

Look at the birds of the air; they do not sow or reap or store away in barns, and yet your Heavenly Father feeds them. Are you not much more valuable than they?

"**I**f I can't have a dog, then I want a duck!" I instantly recognized the voice of my twelve-year-old son coming from the living room, in the all-too-familiar tones used in final negotiations with his mother.

"Mom said I could buy a duck," he continued, as he brought the conversation into the family room to Dad's Chair, where I have pretended for years that all major household decisions are made. "I've done the research at the library and know what to feed it, Grandpa will build a duck house, and all you'll have to do is help me build the pen," he went on, trying to anticipate all the objections my logical mind could concoct. "It will only cost you $1.50" – he brought out the big gun without letting me catch my breath, and the final argument – "and he will guard the house!"

"His cost calculation is right," my accountant's mind mused as we moved toward the van, "if I can convince the hardware store to donate the materials, and the feed store to contribute a lifetime supply of food and straw!" "What will we call this 'guard duck'?" I asked, as we drove to the pet store. "Killer?" "Great idea, Dad," came the reply – convincing me once again that subtle humor is often wasted on a twelve-year-old.

Killer the Guard Duck lived her early life in a "cardboard condo" in our family room, until her cheery "peep" became an adolescent "quack." At that time, she moved into the more luxurious surroundings of Grandpa's Duck House, with its fenced yard and matching curtains.

Killer grew in wisdom and age, learning all those things a boy would teach his dog. She jumped for her food, quacked her thanks, and gathered a curious following of neighborhood children with the slap of webbed feet on concrete as she walked down the sidewalk with her "Mommy." And no one, I was often reminded, ever broke into our house while Killer was on guard!

As the promised two-year lifespan of a Peking duck turned into three, Killer became a noticeable part of our family. Subtly, she began to appear in birthday and graduation photos – but it's still unclear how she managed that weekend in Brown County! Duck jokes multiplied in our house and new words were created. Why have a duck for a pet? The teen-age response: "Cats look down on you and dogs look up to you, but a duck treats you as an equal!" "Killer doesn't pay for her food – she puts it on her bill!" It got worse. "Wibbling" was the word coined to describe the process a duck uses to search for food in the grass. "Quackaphobia" was my contribution: the fear my son would go to college and leave me a duck! When a duck statue appeared in the Christmas manger scene one year, I was sure things had gone too far and protested. "But Dad, it's in the Bible," my son replied. "It says, 'And a duck shall lead them.'" "Paraphrase," I mumbled (you just don't argue when a teen reads the Bible!).

When under stress, I often found myself wandering out to Killer's pen to watch her do "duck things." "Do not be anxious; look at the ducks" seemed an appropriate paraphrase as she contently "wibbled" for her food each day. The shape of her bill seemed to form a perpetual smile as she went about her tasks. "She's always smiling – like she knows something we don't," my son observed. Killer would playfully swim fast laps around her pool, to the delight of the neighborhood kids.

She would then stand up, stretch her neck, flap her wings, and quack in a series, sounding for all the world like she was laughing out loud. "She's happy to be alive and thinks she's lucky to be a duck," my son would say.

One morning, doing what had somehow become "Dad's job" and letting the duck out, with briefcase in hand I approached Killer's house with a cheery "Good morning!" Instead of the quacked response that always started my day with a smile, there was an eerie silence... and I knew that Killer had died.

As we buried Killer, I muttered the question I had once asked as a child: "I wonder if animals go to heaven?" "She's still smiling, Dad," my son noticed. "I still think she knows something we don't." He turned quickly away.

I stayed for my own goodbye. "Thanks for the lessons, Killer. If I could do as well... You brought us joy... and gave glory to your Creator."

Reflection

1. The author tells us that watching "Killer" do her "duck things" – that is, living in the now – was a source of stress relief to him. What does "living in the now" mean? Why is it important to our mental health or happiness?

2. How much of your day is spent living in the now? What can you do to increase this amount?

3. What life lessons did the author learn from "Killer"? What life lessons have you learned from a pet? What might the lessons we learn from our animal friends tell us about our own lives and purposes on earth?

Nice Touch   Mark 5:25-31

There was a woman afflicted with hemorrhages for twelve years. She had suffered much under many physicians, and had spent all that she had, and was no better but rather grew worse. She had heard the reports about Jesus and came up behind him in the crowd and touched his garment. For she said, "If I touch even his garments, I will be made well." And immediately the flow of blood dried up, and she felt in her body that she was healed of her disease. And Jesus, perceiving in himself that power had gone out from him, immediately turned about in the crowd and said, "Who touched my garments?" And his disciples said to him, "You see the crowd pressing around you, and yet you say, 'Who touched me?'"

Sometimes it's the season; sometimes it's a special day, an event, or maybe a place that stimulates moments of reflection. In this case, it was my chance hearing of a remark made by TV personality Dr. Phillip McGraw. "Dr Phil" said that, in our lifetime, we encounter five people who make a difference or permanently influence us. That is, we have five "turning points" or "defining moments" in our lifetime.

I don't know if it was Dr. Phil's remark, but something caused me to stop and reflect on this gospel passage when I came to the part where Jesus asks, "Who touched me?"

I started looking back on my life, and thinking, "Who touched *me?*" Who has made a difference in my life? What were my defining moments? I believe God is in those moments, if the touch is a positive one. I also believe God can redeem those moments if they are negative. I can't explain how it all works. I don't even try to define it – but I certainly believe it.

I find it interesting how people enter our lives. Some do so in a dramatic fashion, while others do so more subtly... but they all leave their mark on us. Sometimes that touch is so subtle that we are not even aware of it, and sometimes years must pass before we can see how it has affected our lives.

My sixth-grade teacher, Mr. Lutton, was my idol. As a kid, I spent hours trying to comb a wave in my hair and put a cleft in my chin, so I would look like Mr. Lutton! Mr. Lutton knew of our struggles at home. He knew that we were a family of seven children being raised by a single parent, and that we were dependent on a paltry welfare check as our sole source of income. With the vision of a born teacher, Mr. Lutton looked past the snot-nosed kid with a hole in his shoe, and saw something more. Mr. Lutton was the first person to encourage me to write. "Someday you'll be an author," he would tell me.

"Who touched me?" Jesus asks... and then he demonstrates how much a touch can change a life.

Mr. Lutton would sometimes pay me for what I wrote. It was his way of helping our family without taking away our pride. Nice touch.

I've been an accountant for most of my professional life. At age fifty-two, I went back to school, earned my Religious Studies degree, and went into ministry. Mr. Lutton was also a minister. Nice touch.

Who has touched *you*? Who has made a difference in your life? Have you ever taken the time to tell them how much they mean to you?

Maybe you should do that. It would be... a nice touch.

Reflection

1. Share three defining moments or turning points in your life. What persons or events were the catalysts for these changes? In what ways do you feel you are now different as a person because of them? How did you experience God in these turning points?

2. Name three people (other than your parents) who have – for good or ill – most significantly influenced your life. Have you ever told them the effect they have had on your life? If not, why haven't you?

3. Name a person who made a difference in your life of which you were unaware at the time. When did you become aware of the effect that person had on your life?

4. What correlations do you see between those people who have influenced you and the life you now lead? Do you see similarities in your priorities and values and those of your significant people?

Here He Comes   Luke 4:33-34

*In the synagogue there was a man with the spirit of
an unclean demon, and he cried out in a loud voice,
"Ha! What have you to do with us, Jesus of Nazareth?
Have you come to destroy us?"*

"Here he comes!" The warning shout always came from
my sister Fran, perched on a limb high in the tallest walnut
tree on our farm. It could have been any Monday morning
in springtime, but it would never be later than eleven o'clock.
The "he" who was coming was our pastor, the Reverend
Father Conrad A. Stoll. That black 1952 Plymouth, first
stopping, then crossing the railroad tracks, was an
unmistakable sign of his coming.

The speed with which Fran descended the walnut tree was
matched only by our brother Paul's bullet-like movement
toward the barn. The girls, meantime, sought the safety of
the house; Father Stoll never went into the house. "If you
had learned your prayers, you wouldn't have to run and hide,"
I shouted at their trails of dust. Even so, I trembled as I
walked toward the driveway, trying to remember the Latin
response to *"Dominus Vobiscum"* and praying that someone
else in town drove a black 1952 Plymouth.

It was a rare scene, Father Stoll wearing something other
than his black cassock and that biretta with the swinging
tassel. Even in his mushroom-picking clothes (purple shirt
and gray slacks), he was a formidable presence to a kid.
"Do you know your prayers?" was Father Stoll's standard
greeting to any child under thirteen. An affirmative answer
called for an impromptu recitation of one or more prayers
from his endless arsenal of "must know to receive communion"
recitations. Boys of altar-serving age were expected

to respond in both English and Latin. It was enough to make a kid hide in the barn!

Just as kids feared the coming of Fr. Stoll, we tremble like the possessed man in this scripture passage when we see Jesus coming... because we know that, when he comes, it will mean a radical change in our lives. It will mean a U-turn or, in military jargon, an "about-face." (In Hebrew scripture, the term used is "*teshuba*.") And so we too cry out, "What do you want of us, Jesus of Nazareth?" I see you coming, you Hound of Heaven, you ever-pursuing one. You come to my door or call to me from the beach. You gaze at me across the fields, and walk toward me in the temple.

"Have you come to destroy us?" Our demons are our comfort and our friends. They have been with us always: those fears that enslave us, those relationships that bind us, those possessions that secure us, the obsessions that control us, and the guilt that clings to us.

We see Jesus coming and we fear his cure more than we fear the demons that possess us.

We see Jesus coming, and we fear what he will ask.

We see Jesus coming, and we fear what he will cast out of us.

We see Jesus coming, and we know that our lives will never be the same.

"Here he comes!"

What will he ask of you today? What demons will *you* allow him to cast out?

Reflection

1. What fears "enslave" you? How could you free yourself from those fears?

2. Has your life been changed by letting go of a fear? How?

3. What is Jesus asking of *you* today? What "demons" do you need him to cast out?

James R. Welter

The Flour Jar   1Kings 17:12-14

(The widow said to the Prophet) "As the LORD, your God, lives," she answered, "I have nothing baked; there is only a handful of flour in my jar and a little oil in my jug. Just now I was collecting a couple of sticks, to go in and prepare something for myself and my son; when we have eaten it, we shall die." "Do not be afraid," Elijah said to her. "Go and do as you propose. But first make me a little cake and bring it to me. Then you can prepare something for yourself and your son. For the LORD, the God of Israel, says, 'The jar of flour shall not go empty, nor the jug of oil run dry, until the day when the LORD sends rain upon the earth.'"

"My idea of heaven," I often tell people, "is an open mike and a captive audience!" Well, I've been in that "heaven" many times since my first book, *When Winter Comes*, was published. I've been invited to give talks to many different groups, and often the topic has been "how to get more out of scripture." One suggestion I make is: when reading scripture, stop at the first word or phrase that jumps out at you, and reflect on that. Following my own suggestion, I didn't have to read very far into this story of Elijah and the widow until I found my key phrase: "The jar of flour shall not go empty..."

In the northern Indiana farmhouse where I grew up, the "jar of flour" was actually an aluminum can... and, when I was a kid, flour was a bit of a mystery to me. The classic question children often ask – "Where do babies come from?" – was not an issue, because we often saw animals being born; birth was a natural part of life on the farm. And it was certainly apparent where most of our food came from: we raised the vegetables, dug the potatoes, picked the apples, collected the eggs, and milked the cows. But I remember once asking my older sister Fran, in a very hushed tone, "Frannie, where does 'flour' come from?"

The white flour can with the bright red lid sat on the first shelf of the cupboard in the house where my mother, as a single parent, raised all seven of us children. That can was, for me, a barometer for our financial situation: there was always hope as long as there was flour in the can. No matter how little food we otherwise had in the house, Mom would say, "Well, I've still got flour; I can make..." The list seemed endless: biscuits, pancakes, dumplings, and more. We could even bake a cake! Smiles all around; we knew we wouldn't go hungry tonight!

But I can still feel the butterflies that swirled in my stomach whenever I heard the words, "We're out of flour; the can is empty!" *That* put us in "survival mode." It usually meant a mile-long walk across two fields, over the creek, and down the road to see if Mrs. Springs had any flour we could borrow. In this passage, scripture reminds us that "the jar of flour will not go empty"... as long as we love. "The jug of oil will not go dry"... as long as we share.

The "jar of flour" is that inner strength upon which we draw during difficult times; it is that inner fortitude that sustains us when we have nowhere else to turn. It is the sum of our life experiences: the relationships we form, the love we receive, and the faith we share. It is the prayers said and the prayers received. It is the strength we are given and the hope we rely on.

"Frannie, where does flour come from?" I asked. She laughed when I didn't believe her story about the wheat in the field and the process that ground it into powder. I started to cry.

She put her arm around me.

"Flour," she said, "comes from those who love us."

Reflection

1. What are some of the symbols from your past and what images or feelings do they generate in your life today?

2. What past experiences in your life still cause you tension or give you "butterflies"? How do those feelings effect your actions today?

3. From what images, experiences or beliefs do you draw strength during difficult times?

Abundant God   ***Mark 8:18-19***

And do you not remember, when I broke the five loaves for the five thousand, how many baskets of fragments you picked up?" They answered him, "Twelve." He said to them, "Do you still not understand?"

"Hobo" isn't a word you hear much anymore; it has gone the way of smokestacks and train whistles in the night. But when I was growing up, the Nickel Plate railroad ran through the farm where we lived. There was just a small field between our house and the railroad tracks – and you could actually set your clock by the passing of the trains.

One day, when I was about eight years old, a "hobo" jumped off a slow-moving train and came to our house to ask for food. Our family was poor, but from my hiding place, I could hear Mom's response: "We don't have much, but we'll share what we have." She then made him a sandwich and gave him a jar of water, and he was on his way. I came out of my hiding place in tears. "You gave our food away! Now what will we have to eat?" "God knows we're hungry," she said, as she put her arm around me. "We'll have enough."

In this scripture passage, the apostles once again don't "get it," so Jesus tries to help them understand the deeper meaning of the miracle he has performed. Our God is a God of abundance; everyone is fed and there are baskets left over – enough to feed "all of God's people" (symbolized in Hebrew numerology by the number twelve).

Our God is a God of abundance, yet we often live in a "scarcity" mentality. All we can see is what we lack, what we need, and what we want. The focus is not on God and his ability to provide, but rather on us and our scarcity. Jesus' reminder

that there will be "baskets left over" is superseded by our fears about our jobs, mortgage payments, college tuition, food, clothing, shelter, and luxuries. We cling tightly to the things we have, including our time, our abilities, our money, and our resources. We seem to believe that if we let go of them or "use them up," we will have nothing left.

But we have a lavish and generous God – a God of abundance! God always gives us more than we need; there are always "baskets left over." Yet we still live in fear, and hoard what we've been given. We choose to live in scarcity; we live as if there isn't enough, and so others go without.

When I think of Purgatory – that is, the purging or cleansing that takes place as we pass from this life to the next – I think of it as the pain and emptiness we will feel when we become fully aware of our lost potential. I think of it as a time when God will show us all the good we could have done, and did not do; all the lives we could have touched had we fully used our gifts and had more faith. I think of it as the painful realization of all the wonderful things we could have accomplished if we had really believed in an abundant God and had not chosen to live out of fear and scarcity – of the remarkable difference we could have made with our lives had we only trusted in God for our daily bread and truly believed that there would be "baskets left over."

Confronted with such a revelation, which of us would not repent in the words of the ancient Islamic prayer: "For all I should have said, and have not said; for all I should have done, and have not done; for all I should have been, and have not been... I beg you, O Lord, for forgiveness"?

Now is our chance to act.

As the "hobo" steps off the train...

How will you express your belief in an "abundant God" today?

Reflection

1. What gift or talent could you be using more fully?   How might you do so?

2. What mentality of "scarcity" exists in your life?   How might you be able to overcome it?

3. "God always gives us more than we need." Have you experienced this in your life? How? Do you think this is true for everyone? Why or why not?

4. What could you do (that you are not currently doing) if you really believed that there would be "baskets left over"?

The Church in the Wildwood   Luke 17:11-16

On the way to Jerusalem he was passing along between Samaria and Galilee. And as he entered a village, he was met by ten lepers, who stood at a distance and lifted up their voices, saying, "Jesus, Master, have mercy on us." When he saw them he said to them, "Go and show yourselves to the priests." And as they went they were cleansed. Then one of them, when he saw that he was healed, turned back, praising God with a loud voice; and he fell on his face at the feet of Jesus, and thanked him.

It was a rite of spring for our family. Each Memorial Day, all seven of us would walk from our farm to the Eagle Creek cemetery to decorate the grave of our infant sister, Jeanette, who had died years before. The trip was long for us young children, and my oldest sister Dot would often help pass the time by identifying the farmhouses we passed along the way. "There's where the Rodgers' live; they have a tractor... Billy Lane, the cute boy from school, lives in that house by the creek... the house down there is where the Brems live." The final landmark was the old one-room schoolhouse across the road from the cemetery.

One year, when we visited the cemetery, the gate was locked. That was no obstacle for my tomboy sister, Fran – she would sometimes climb over the fence even when the gate was open! There was a little white church beside the cemetery, just across a gravel drive from Jeanette's grave. As a child, I was sure it was the "church in the wildwood" mentioned in that song my mother sometimes sang. "See that white church over there?" Fran said to me one day. "They're the ones that bring us presents at Christmas."

Mom raised seven of us on a farm just two miles from that church and cemetery. Mom was all alone – there was no

electricity on the farm, no running water, no telephone or nearby neighbors. But during those years, we could always count on the ladies from the Eagle Creek Church to remember us at Christmas. From our hiding place, we would hear the ladies tell Mom, "We just brought a few things for the children." And we knew that Santa would come this year!

How could those ladies have known that their "few things" *were* our Christmas celebration? How could we have known that, one day, both Mom and Fran would lie beside Jeanette in the cemetery just across the gravel drive from that little white church?

In this passage from the gospel of Luke, Jesus is distressed because only one person who was cured returned to give thanks. And he asks, "Where are the other nine?" (Luke 17:17) We can answer that question... because *we* are the other nine! We are the other nine when we fail to say "thank you" to those who have touched our lives, lifted our spirits, or helped us to carry our burden.

Each Sunday evening, the good people at the Eagle Creek Church gather to give praise and sing some of the old gospel songs that my mother knew so well. I was invited to their gathering one Sunday, to share some reflections from my first book, *When Winter Comes*. What a blessing it was for me to stand before that group and say "thank you" for the kindness they showed us all those years ago.

After a short reception, when lights were out and the cars were gone... I crossed the gravel drive and went over to the cemetery. The gate was open, but I climbed over the fence – Fran would've understood. And I sat on the ground next to her grave and looked back across the gravel drive, at that "church in the wildwood."

"Frannie, do you see that white church over there?" I whispered. "I told them 'thank you' today."

Reflection

1. What person or group has touched your life in a significant way? Have you "returned" to thank them?

2. Why do we so often find it difficult (or perhaps even neglect) to say "thank you" to someone?

3. What are the risks of "returning" to give thanks? How can we deal with those risks?

4. Reflect upon a memory from your childhood of Christians living their faith. What has it taught you? How has it affected your life?

Follow Me   Matthew 9:9

As Jesus passed on from there, he saw a man called Matthew sitting at the tax booth, and he said to him, "Follow me." And he rose and followed him.

The invitation sounds so simple: "Follow me."

Jesus didn't say "institutionalize me." He didn't say "dogmatize me," or "argue about me," or "define me." In fact, he didn't say to do a lot of the things that we usually do in connection with him. No, he simply said, "Follow me"!

Following Jesus is about... well... it's about *following!* It's about movement. It's about purpose. It's about a journey we haven't taken: days that haven't happened, people we haven't met, places we haven't gone, forgiveness we haven't given or asked for – yet.

Following Jesus starts *today* – from wherever you are at this very moment. *Now* is the time. Clinging to the security of yesterday's answers is never enough. Telling yesterday's story and polishing yesterday's truths are never enough.

Follow me!

"Faith is a journey," Jesus would say to us. It will take you beyond yesterday's memories, beyond yesterday's understanding. It will take you beyond your "comfort zone," beyond the familiar, and beyond your desire for control. Faith is about action and movement. Faith is a road you travel, not a destination you reach.

Follow me!

On this journey you will see new things, just as I promised! You will hear new words, and reconsider your old words. You will meet new companions, and they will challenge you. You will experience new needs that will require you to

abandon your former ways of perceiving and understanding the world.

Follow me!

You will sometimes feel tongue-tied and confused. You will often feel rootless and unsettled. And that is how I want you to be, for you are on a journey. Only then can you share Abraham's journey, to a land he had never seen. Only then can you journey with Moses, to a land that existed only as a promise. Only then can you journey with me... to a hill outside the city, beyond your sight. And to the unimagined places beyond that.

Follow me.

Many of my disciples defied the wisdom of their day and left everything to follow me. Many gave up their work, their fortunes... their entire lives as they had known them.

Follow me.

I will change your priorities. I will ask for a level of trust and faith that will challenge and test you. I will ask you to pick up your cross. It will never be easy. And there will be no easier or better time to start your journey than now.

Follow me.

Follow me to forgiveness.

Follow me to love.

Follow me to life.

Every journey begins with a single step.

Will you take that step today?

Reflection

1. In what circumstances or time in your life did your faith journey begin? How has it developed since then?

2. Name some of the major events, people and places that have had a significant impact on your spiritual journey.

3. What are some of the new things you have seen, challenges you have faced, and experiences you've had on your faith journey? How have they affected you?

Living in the Mist   Mark 6:53-56

After making the crossing, they came to land at Gennesaret and tied up there. As they were leaving the boat, people immediately recognized him. They scurried about the surrounding country and began to bring in the sick on mats to wherever they heard he was. Whatever villages or towns or countryside he entered, they laid the sick in the marketplaces and begged him that they might touch only the tassel on his cloak; and as many as touched it were healed.

"Writing is easy," a creative writing instructor once told me. "All you have to do is stare at the paper until little drops of blood form on your forehead!" I remembered that quote as I struggled to write a reflection based on this scripture passage. It's a troubling passage: "and as many as touched it (his cloak) were healed." The gospel commentary I sometimes use to stimulate my thoughts says, "We need only be humble enough to ask and to receive."

But that statement raises more questions than it answers! We all pray for good things: we pray for a good job so we can provide for our family, we pray for the safety of our children, we pray for peace in the world, we pray that others may come to faith. And in the Eucharist, we touch far more than the tassel of Jesus' cloak; we receive his very body and blood! Yet often, it seems, we are not healed. It appears that we ask, but do not receive.

My wife, Helen, is a hospice nurse. In recent months, she has cared for an unusually high number of young people who were suffering from cancer. Most of them had families, and several had small children. Many of them prayed; some of them "touched the tassel of his cloak" in the Eucharist. But all of them died. I'm also reminded that, in the book of Acts,

Stephen prayed while being stoned, but the rocks still flew. Jesus also prayed, but the cup did not pass.

Why do young people die? Why do the innocent suffer? Why does it have to be this way? We all ask these questions... but no one has the answer. Living without the answers – living in the mist, living in the question – is perhaps the greatest challenge of our faith. Why can't this cup pass? Why must good people endure misfortune, suffer, and die? According to Luke's gospel, Jesus struggled with that question until little drops of blood *literally* formed on his forehead.

It was our first morning in the Canadian Rockies, and my wife and I were riding the lift up to the highest peak in Banff National Park. The scene was supposed to be spectacular, but we had gotten up late that morning and the fog had already set in. The mist was so thick that we couldn't even see the 5,000-foot mountain right in front of us! "This is a waste of money!" I exclaimed. (My accountant's mind tends to reduce things to dollars and cents.) "We might as well go back down." "Well, we're here now," my wife replied. "We might as well have a cup of coffee." (Helen usually finds a positive side in these things.) There was a long boardwalk there connecting two mountain peaks, and as we proceeded along that boardwalk with coffee cups in hand (which is as close as I get to "hiking"), the mist parted and revealed a lush, beautiful green valley. We could see the town far below us, and a river meandering through the lowlands. The scene only lasted for a moment before the mist concealed it once more. Then, behind us, a towering snow-capped mountain appeared. For over an hour, the scenes kept changing as the wind moved the clouds of mist, hiding one scene only to reveal another. In such a setting, one is naturally moved to prayer. The message felt so profound: faith is living in the mist! We live in the mist every day, and we must trust that God

will reveal that which we cannot see. We must have faith that God will walk with us in the valley, and that, in his good time, he will show us the mountaintop.

God is in the mist. Be at peace.

Reflection

1. In what areas of your life are you "living in the mist" or "living in the question"?

2. Think of some situations in which you prayed and your prayers (apparently) were not answered. How do you explain your good and selfless prayers not being answered?

3. What effect does God's silence have on your life? How has it affected your faith?

4. What difference has prayer made in your life? On what occasions do you think your prayers may have been "answered" in ways different from those you expected?

Going to Cleveland   Matthew 10:34-35

"Do not think that I have come to bring peace upon the earth. I have come to bring not peace but the sword. For I have come to set a man against his father, a daughter against her mother, and a daughter-in-law against her mother-in-law..."

It was a long day at the airport in South Bend, Indiana. We had been there for five hours, waiting for the thunderstorms to pass so we could go to a wedding in Cleveland. At last we were allowed to board the plane. Storm clouds and darkness were visible on one side of the plane, but on the other side, the sun had broken through. Just then, the voice of the pilot came over the intercom: "It's open seating; you can choose to look at the darkness or you can choose to look at the light. But either way... this plane is going to Cleveland!"

The above scripture passage, which is taken from the gospel of Matthew, isn't very "warm and fuzzy." In fact, it's not very comforting at all! "For I have come to set a man against his father, a daughter against her mother..." As if the people of Israel don't have enough problems being bullied and oppressed by the Romans, now Jesus says he has come to bring division and enmity within families. It makes you wonder how he got the title "Prince of Peace"!

I often say that one of the blessings of getting older is the realization that we don't have unlimited time left; this insight gives us a sense of urgency in living. Usually around age fifty, there comes a realization that we have to prioritize our lives – we have to decide what is truly important and make some tough choices. In her work in hospice, my wife often reminds her patients that, even in dying, they still have choices: to continue or stop treatment, to reconcile relationships, to write letters, to share their wisdom with

their children and grandchildren. They can choose to plan their own funeral and convey the ways in which they want to be remembered.

Many events in life force us to make choices: loss of a job, a divorce, an illness, various physical limitations, or a death. Few would willingly choose these painful experiences, yet it is often through them that we grow and become more fully alive. It is frequently through such unpleasant happenings that we have the opportunity to become more sensitive, more caring, and more *human*. We may even become aware of gifts and talents buried deep within, which we would otherwise never have discovered. We can't choose or control much of what happens to us in life, but we *can* choose how we will respond to the situations in which we find ourselves.

No matter what we choose, life will go on.

Either way... this plane is going to Cleveland!

In this scripture passage, Jesus tells us that, to follow him, we must make choices. He challenges us to give up our mundane lives and surface security, and to make a commitment to something larger than ourselves. Security makes it too easy to just "do what we've always done," without thinking. Jesus didn't come to continue the status quo – he came to shake things up! He came to cause division, to motivate re-thinking, and to force choices.

Jesus is always offering us choices: choose God or money, choose revenge or forgiveness, choose love or hate, choose self or others. Choosing between two ways or roads is a common theme in Hebrew scripture as well, and Jesus frequently draws on those themes. In this passage, he echoes the challenge of Moses (Deut 30:19): "I set before

you life and death..." Jesus is radical in this passage; he tells us to leave our families, our homes, our jobs – leave everything that is safe and secure – and follow him.

Jesus and Moses both remind us that we always have choices! In effect, Jesus says to us: "I set before you life and death. You can choose to be selfish or generous... kind or mean-spirited... forgiving or vengeful... helpful to others or harmful to them... loving or hateful. You can choose life, or you can choose death."

And like that airline pilot, he might well add: "Either way... this plane is going to Cleveland!"

Reflection

1. What is the most difficult choice you have ever had to make in your life? How was that choice resolved?

2. What process do you go through when you have a difficult choice to make?

3. Besides the decision to get married, remain single, or have children, what has been your most significant choice?

4. What choices in your life do you regret making? Why?

5. Discuss the statement that "we always have choices." Do you agree with this statement? Why or why not? What do you think Jesus might say about this statement?

Come Next Spring

James R. Welter

Love is Patient, Love is Kind
1 Corinthians 13:4-7,13

Love is patient and kind; love does not envy or boast; it is not arrogant or rude. It does not insist on its own way; it is not irritable or resentful; it does not rejoice at wrongdoing, but rejoices with the truth. Love bears all things, believes all things, hopes all things, endures all things. In the end only three things matter: faith, hope, and love, these three; but the greatest of these is love.

An often-sung hymn in Catholic congregations includes the line: "We are many parts / we are all one body / and the gifts we have / we are given to share." That song is based on St. Paul's first letter to the Corinthians, in which he is addressing the universal problem of factions within the community. "There are many parts but only one body," he writes (1Cor 12:12). I think the operative word here is "parts." Problems arise in the Church and in our lives when we begin to believe that we are the whole "body," rather than just *part* of it. We start making claims that *our* part of the body is somehow the whole body, and we begin to think and act as if our way is the *only* way. We begin to feel as though everyone must echo *our* views, take part in *our* rituals, and endorse *our* form of spirituality – or they will be cut off and cast away!

Paul continues his letter to the Corinthians with some of the most beautiful lines in scripture, reminding us all that "love is patient, love is kind..." And while those poetic words are certainly ideal for cross-stitched pillows and wedding celebrations, I think Paul had something much more challenging in mind when he wrote them.

Charity is a lot tougher than we like to admit. Maybe all those cross-stitched pillows and "precious moments" sentiments

76

have clouded our vision, because the charity that Paul later speaks of is an invitation into the paschal mystery. It is an invitation into the heart of what it means to be a Christian. It will involve dying: to ourselves, to our wants, to our plans, to our dreams. But it involves rising, too – rising to the Lord's call to love. And it includes loving all those other "parts" of the "body," even those we find difficult. It includes loving those obnoxious "parts" that don't have the grace to see things our way, those "parts" that annoy us and challenge us, those "parts" that hurt us and have yet to ask for forgiveness.

"In the end," Paul continues in his letter to the Corinthians, "only three things matter: faith, hope and love... but the greatest of these is love." Love remains our source and our strength; love never fails. In the community, love washes away the indifference between us. Love expresses itself in listening to the story hidden in someone's heart, and opening our heart to them. Love sustains us with the knowledge that we are not alone, and reminds us that each moment is a gift.

Love makes sense of it all.

Love makes life worth living.

Love connects us to each other.

Love... leads us to God.

Reflection

1. What "part" of the body of Christ are you?   What talents or gifts do you offer to your church or faith community?

2. In what areas of your life (or what person/people) do you find it difficult to love? Why?

3. In your opinion, what is "at the heart of being a Christian"? How can you best live that out?

Turning the Tables   John 2:13-15

The Passover of the Jews was at hand, and Jesus went up to Jerusalem. In the temple he found those who were selling oxen and sheep and pigeons, and the money-changers sitting there. And making a whip of cords, he drove them all out of the temple, with the sheep and oxen. And he poured out the coins of the money-changers and overturned their tables.

We called them the "Did I's": they constituted a list of sins in the 1950s Baltimore Catechism that was designed to help children prepare for confession. There were pages and pages of them, and the list was exhaustive: "Did I lie? Did I steal? Did I eat meat on Friday? Did I get angry?"

Back then, anger was always considered a sin. No distinctions were made about what caused our anger, or how it was expressed or acted out. It was never suggested that anger is a natural emotion and necessary for our emotional wellbeing. Small wonder that we so quickly jump on this scripture passage to defend ourselves when we get angry, saying "Look, even Jesus got angry!"

But to focus on Jesus' anger in this passage is to miss the point. This passage isn't about Jesus getting angry – it's about Jesus believing that the Temple was more than just a building. It's about Jesus trying to overturn preconceived ideas, trying to get people to "think outside the box." When Jesus says "Destroy *this* temple, and in three days, I'll rebuild it," the Pharisees take him literally and respond from their preconceived idea of a temple. "It took 46 years to build this temple," they laugh, referring to the massive stone structure, "and you're going to rebuild it in three days?!" But that's not what Jesus meant. They don't get it!

79

If we think this scripture passage is about Jesus getting angry – or that it's only about the Pharisees' narrow vision – then we don't get it either!

St. Paul says, "Do you not know that *you* are God's temple?"(1Cor 3:16).

It is in *this* temple that Jesus wants to be seen. It is in *this* temple that he will overturn tables. So let's get out of our box and into the story. Let's imagine that Jesus is visiting *our* "temple" today. No doubt we could show him some beautiful rooms in our temple: we could share with him our feelings of care, sympathy, and love. We could mention our forgiving moments, and show him examples of unselfish giving.

But let's look beyond those comfortable places, and take him to that room where he has not yet been; where we have not *allowed* him to go. That room is the part of our heart we've guarded, saying, "No! I won't change *that!*" "No one will get in *there.*" Yet it is only in *this* place that we can truly encounter Jesus. It is the part of us that is shielded from love, protected from what Jesus might ask of us. It is that place, in our heart and in our life, where we say, "Yes, Lord, you can have anything *but...*" "I'll love everyone *except...*" "I'll be generous *until...*" "I'll forgive *if...*" "I'll follow you *as long as...*"

This is the area of the temple that Jesus would visit. *These* are the tables he would overturn and the moneychangers he would drive out!

Will you invite Jesus into your temple today?

Reflection

1. What injustice, hurt or betrayal in your life still makes you angry or causes resentment?

2. What "tables" in your life would Jesus overturn? Think of a negative feeling that you continue to harbor. Is it hurt? Resentment? Jealousy? Some injury that you have not forgiven?

3. Is there an area of your life that you are not able to share? Spend some time there with Jesus this week. How long has this "room" in your "temple" been closed to the rest of the world? How do its contents affect your life?

Live in the Promise   Numbers 21:9

Moses accordingly made a bronze serpent and mounted it on a pole, and whenever anyone who had been bitten by a serpent looked at the bronze serpent, he lived.

Serpents were plaguing the chosen people as they wandered in the desert, and "many of them were bitten and died." (Num 21:6) So Moses prayed, and God told him to make an image of a serpent and mount it on a pole. "Moses accordingly made a bronze serpent and mounted it on a pole, and whenever anyone who had been bitten by a serpent looked at the bronze serpent, he lived."

Looking at death gives life.

In scripture, Jesus talks about salvation and about being saved from our sins. To make his point, he draws on the book of Numbers: "And as Moses lifted up the serpent in the wilderness, so must the Son of Man be lifted up, that whoever believes in him may have eternal life" (John 3:14-15). To give us life, Jesus is lifted up on a cross. And like the Israelites, we must gaze upon him who has been raised up, and believe, and we too will be saved from death.

Looking at death gives life.

We witness the paradox of life coming from death with every flower that blooms and with every tree that grows. It is the very rhythm of life – yet we often resist the flow and, in the words of Dylan Thomas, we "do not go gentle into that good night." We resist the change. We resist the letting go. We resist the dying that is essential for our growth. How often we pray to be excluded from the trials of life! How often we ask God to "make this disease go away," "exempt me from suffering," "help my child," "save my spouse," "find me a job," "make my life easier." Yet looking at Jesus raised up on the

cross reminds us that we too must let go; that we too must go through the dying.

And it is in our dying that we are given new life.

When looking at death, we sometimes appreciate life more, and hold our loved ones just a little closer. I know cancer survivors who have stared death in the face, and who now embrace life as a very precious gift, not taking even an ordinary sunrise for granted.

For me, turning fifty came with a realization that my time was not unlimited. This created a sense of urgency in living and caused me to re-prioritize many things. Looking at the "death" of a job led me to make new decisions and do things I never dreamed possible.

Looking at death gives life.

Our dying takes many forms. There is a dying when a loved one is suddenly gone. There is a dying when we lose a job, or when relationships change. There is a dying when we go through a divorce, or a longtime friend moves away. There is a dying when our health fails, or our aging bodies weaken.

It is good for us to grieve these losses, and even revisit them from time to time, to allow ourselves to acknowledge the hurt and feel the pain. And it is here, in the pain and the frustration of our lives – in our everyday dying and letting go – that Jesus asks us to look at him raised on the cross. It is here, looking at death, that we are given the promise of new life. It is here that everything is made new. It is here, looking at death, that we must let go and say "yes" to life.

Looking at death gives life.

Live in the promise!

Reflection

1. List three things you would do if you knew that you had only six months to live. To the extent you are comfortable doing so, share your list with others.

2. Put a "to do" date on each item on your list. Place the list in an envelope and review it each year on this date.

3. Letting Go:

> **a.** Make a list of the ten most important things in your life. You may list people, things you own, things you want to do or accomplish, or places you want go.

> **b.** You must now let go of two things on your list. Mark off those two items.

> **c.** Reflect on your experience of choosing those two items.

> **d.** Now you must let go of two more things.

> **e.** Reflect on your feelings of choosing these two items.

> **f.** You now have six items remaining on your list. Continue the process by marking off two more items. Is it getting more difficult?

> **g.** Now you are down to four items. The decisions are getting even more difficult. Are you beginning to feel like a dying person who must finally let go of everything?

> **h.** When you have only two items remaining, choose one to mark from your list.

> **i.** What was the last thing remaining? You have chosen this as the most important thing in your life. Consider how you feel about letting go of this final item.

Did this exercise help you to better understand the dying process? What do the choices you made, or the order in which you made them, say about the priorities in your life?

Moving On   *Luke 9:51-56*

When the days drew near for him to be taken up, he set his face to go to Jerusalem. And he sent messengers ahead of him, who went and entered a village of the Samaritans, to make preparations for him. But the people did not receive him, because his face was set toward Jerusalem. And when his disciples James and John saw it, they said, "Lord, do you want us to call fire down from heaven and consume them?" But he turned and rebuked them. And they journeyed to another village.

My younger brother, Harold, says there are only two kinds of music in the world: country and western! This gospel passage brings to mind the words of a Kenny Rogers song (he's a country singer, for those of you who don't share my brother's tastes): "Know when to hold 'um / know when to fold 'um / know when to walk away / and know when to run."

James and John are hurt and angry at the rejection they receive in a Samaritan village, and they want to lash out. "Shall we call fire down upon them?" they ask. But Jesus knew that, if the disciples remained in their anger, *they* would be the ones consumed. So instead, he tells them to walk away, to move on: "And they journeyed to another village." There are times to stay and persist, and there are times to "move on to another village."

Moving on is one of life's great survival skills. A relationship fails, or no longer works? Move on. Make a bad investment, or a business deal goes sour? Move on. Fail at a task, or lose an opportunity? Move on. Want to put the past behind you, or get more from life? Move on.

Moving on is more than just a survival skill; moving on is essential to our mental, emotional, and spiritual health.

Too often we "get stuck." We get stuck in old ideas or in destructive relationships; we get stuck in our past and in our prejudices. We get stuck in grief. Sometimes we get stuck in faded dreams, or the learned behaviors of our earlier life situations. We may find ourselves paralyzed or imprisoned by our own attitudes and behaviors, by other people, or by situations beyond our control. And the answer, as Jesus suggests, is often simply to move on to "another village."

Moving on doesn't necessarily mean abandoning one's life or jettisoning other people. The answer to a troubled relationship or difficult situation isn't always to pack a bag. Moving on can simply mean leaving behind whatever self-defeating behavior, stored-up resentment, or negative attitude that has contributed to our bad circumstances. Moving on might mean joining hands and moving forward together. In any case, though, standing still isn't an option. "Moving on" always means change.

Jesus kept his eye on the goal – "He set his face to go to Jerusalem." He didn't let the rejection of the villagers or the anger of his friends distract him. He simply moved on.

Moving on always means going to a new place – not the tried and true, or the safe and secure, but somewhere farther. Moving toward a promise. Moving toward our "Jerusalem." Moving on with Jesus, dreaming of wholeness in the midst of brokenness, and life in the midst of death.

With Jesus, every day is "moving day."

How will you "move on" with him today?

Reflection

1. In what situation in your life do you need to "move on" from? What kind of move will this be? A physical move? A change in attitude? A value re-assessment?

2. What makes this move difficult for you?

3. How might your life be different after this move?

4. What support will you have to help you with this move, and the changes it will bring?

5. In your life decisions, how do you decide when to "hold 'um" and when to "fold 'um"? In other words, how do you decide when to "dig in" and when to move on? What are some guidelines that can help make that decision clear, or at least reasonable?

They Were Fishermen   Matthew 4:18

While walking by the Sea of Galilee, he saw two brothers, Simon (who is called Peter) and Andrew his brother, casting a net into the sea, for they were fishermen.

It is often the little tidbits of information in the gospels that put a human face on the stories and help us identify with the characters. Sometimes those seemingly unimportant bits of information can speak volumes, as in this passage.

"They were fishermen."

Those three words tell us that Jesus chooses very ordinary people to bring about God's kingdom. Those who were chosen to walk with Christ were not professionals; they had no wealth, no social position, no exceptional education, and no special advantages. They were selected from among common people who did ordinary things – "they were fishermen"! Yet Jesus chose them.

They were weak!

He chose those who would deny him. I deny Jesus every time I choose a false god – wealth, power, fame, or popularity. I deny Jesus when I allow my job or my need for security or possessions to be first in my life. He chooses those who deny him, like Simon Peter... like me.

They were violent!

He chose zealots, those who resort to violence to deal with problems. I often respond in kind when I'm injured or treated unfairly. Sometimes my actions hurt my family, my neighbor, or my co-workers. He chooses those who resort to violence, like Judas... like me.

They were ambitious!

He chose ambitious people, those who "look out for number one." I have angled for the biggest desk and the corner office with the view; I have fought for promotions, raises, and titles. I have put my job before my family; I have slighted a colleague for my own advantage. He chooses ambitious people, like the Sons of Zebedee... like me.

They were dishonest!

He chose the tax collectors, those who take advantage of the less fortunate. I often buy the cheapest item, without regard for the unjust labor that brought it to me. Sometimes I agree to be "paid in cash" to avoid my share of the tax. Other times I "forget" to fill in that line on the form that would send more of my money to fund programs for the poor. He chooses tax collectors, like Matthew... like me.

They were doubters!

He chose those who doubted. I have the need to take control, to be in charge and "make things happen." In my desperate self-reliance, I doubt that God is aware of my needs or will take care of them; I doubt that he will help me. He chooses those who doubt, like Thomas... like me.

They are *us!*

It is such as us – imperfect, ordinary people – whom God sends out to proclaim the presence of his kingdom and to help those who are in need and are suffering. Obviously, God doesn't choose us because we are denying, violent, ambitious, greedy, or doubting! Maybe God simply sees in us what we oftentimes do not see in ourselves: our courage, our

faithfulness, our enthusiasm, our persistence, our sincerity... our willingness to keep on trying.

God does not choose us for who we are – God chooses us for what we are capable of becoming.

What is God calling you to "become" today?

Reflection

1. How does it make you feel to know that Jesus chose someone like you to follow him? How does it challenge you?

2. What must you do to become all that Jesus believes you can be?

3. What have you learned about yourself in recent years? How do you see yourself differently today than you did years ago?

4. What effect have you had in someone's life that has surprised you?

Hand on the Plow   Luke 9:59-63

To another he said, "Follow me." But he said, "Lord,
let me first go and bury my father." And Jesus said to
him, "Let the dead bury the dead. But as for you, go
and proclaim the kingdom of God." Yet another said,
"I will follow you, Lord, but let me first say farewell
to those at my home." Jesus said to him, "No one who
puts his hand to the plow and looks back is fit for the
kingdom of God."

It's a spring morning in the 1940s. The birds are still singing,
yet two of my sisters and I have already chosen the tree that
would give us shade. Our spot must be in sight of the horse
and plow, so Dad can watch our comings and goings as he
plows the field. Already we are too near the railroad tracks,
but the chance to see a railroad motorcar up close is too much
for our childhood curiosity.

The railroad men are gathering at the nearby crossing; they
will soon be taken by motorcar to the section of track they
will be repairing today. "Your father will never finish plowing
that field in one day," the foreman shouts as we approach the
motorcar. The birds flutter from the trees with the first loud
noise of the morning. "Yes, he will!" we reply. "Our Daddy
can do anything!" A crying protest, and our father comes
running – and a teasing comment becomes an adult
confrontation. As the motorcar moves away, my father gets
in the last word: "By the time you get back at 4 o'clock, this
field will be finished!"

Sniffles reveal a child's disbelief. "All we have is one horse.
How will we do that, Daddy?" His reply is strong and confident.
"We will keep our hand on the plow, and not look back!"

"Keep your hand on the plow; don't look back," my father
would caution again and again throughout the day as each of

us took our turn "helping." If you looked back using a walking plow, your furrow would be crooked. You had to look straight ahead in order to keep the plow from going off course.

The directive to not look back is given early in scripture, with the story of Lot's wife (Gen 19:17). It is reiterated strongly in the New Testament, when a would-be follower of Jesus asks for a favor – "First let me bury my father" – and Jesus replies, "Let the dead bury the dead."

By this comment, Jesus appears insensitive to a Jew's sacred duty to ensure a decent burial for a dead parent. But the ancient Jews used the phrase "I must bury my father" as verbal shorthand for the conventional wisdom that a son should complete all duties to parents and relatives before leaving home. In other words, the young man wanted to put off following Jesus for an "easier" and "less disruptive" time: "I'll follow you as soon as I get my affairs in order; just let me bury my father."

But Jesus understood the tragedy of the un-seized moment. He knew this young man was at a turning point, a defining moment in his life, and he realized that if this man didn't leave now, he would *never* leave his familiar life. He would be forever shackled by expectations and responsibilities, a prisoner of his own "comfort zone." And thus the reply, "Let the dead bury the dead!" Let those who are spiritually "dead" – to opportunity, to new experiences, to themselves – let those numbed souls give themselves over to everyday concerns! As for *you*: follow me!

And the disciple who wanted to "say farewell to those at home" was just doing what we all do: tapping home plate before swinging the bat, verifying "here" before going "there." He was validating himself as capable of movement. But, like us, he was approaching Jesus with conditions.

So Jesus says "no" to these requests. He allows no conditions, no stalling, no foot-dragging, no second-guessing. It's now or never; you're either in or you're out.

Now are you in, he asks... or are you out?

At one level, his response makes good sense; you can't plow a field while looking back. But at another level, it reveals the "madness" of faith. Jesus appealed to the would-be followers' heart and told them to detach themselves from whatever might keep them from following. He tells them, in effect, that if you're still clinging to something, you're not ready. If you're looking back, you haven't escaped – you haven't really "left" at all. "When you put your hand to the plow, don't look back." That's what surrender means; that's what commitment means. That's what following Jesus means.

When we decide to put our hand on the plow and "not look back," we must do so in faith. At that moment, there is no more research to do, no more books to read, no more counseling to seek. There are no more questions to ask, and no hand to hold.

There is only God.

Looking back is an attempt to stay in control. It's the ultimate addiction, the last illusion we will relinquish – the last temptation we will face. It is, in a sense, our "last defense" against God.

Being left only with God can be a difficult and fearful thing. What if God's answer isn't what I want to hear? What if God asks me for something I don't want to give? What if my searching – my not looking back – brings me to a road I haven't walked before?

James R. Welter

By not looking back, we are going beyond simply preparing ourselves for change – we are being prepared for new life and new growth. We are the ground being plowed, the furrow being turned. We are in every follower's shoes. We don't know where the road is going, but we must put our trust in The Way.

"Don't look back" is the Lord's counsel in all movements of life: leaving neighborhoods, changing jobs, starting new careers, beginning new relationships, or accepting the death of loved ones. "Don't look back" doesn't mean that we deny our past, but only that we don't *live* out of it. To "live out of my past" is to be controlled by time and events that no longer exist. "Don't look back" is God's invitation to live in the *now*... which is the only time we have.

"Here it comes!" The late afternoon sun was low in the sky when my sister Fran sounded the warning that the returning motorcar was in sight. My father had just finished the last furrow, and left the horse in the field to run to our side. The motorcar rolled to a stop as the boisterous man began his apology. "You got it finished!" he exclaimed, his voice softer now. "Francie" – my father's German accent seemed thicker than usual – "Francie, tell dem how we did it!"

My six-year old sister's voice was barely audible:

"We kept our hand on the plow... and didn't look back!"

Reflection

1. When in your life have you been challenged to "keep your hand on the plow and not look back"? How did the situation turn out?

2. Talk about a time in your life when you put off doing what you knew you were being called to do? How did you resolve your procrastination?

3. What does it mean to you to follow Jesus? What concerns must you "put aside" in order to do so?

My Father's Hand   John 10:27,29

*My sheep hear my voice; I know them, and they
follow me. I give them eternal life, and they shall
never perish. My Father, who has given them to me,
is greater than all, and no one can take them out of
my Father's hand.*

This gospel passage is both a comfort and a challenge.
The poetic words of John echo the promise of Easter:
"My sheep hear my voice. I know them... I give them eternal
life, they shall never perish... and no one can take them out of
my Father's hand."

As Christians, we have every right to feel safe and secure in
God's love, because these words are spoken to us. But there
is also a part of this passage that bothers me! The line "my
sheep hear my voice" makes me a little uneasy, because I
know it's the same voice that called Lazarus from the darkness
of the tomb. It's the same voice that challenged Peter to step
out of the boat! In that story, Peter hears the voice of Jesus
and steps out of his boat and begins walking on the water –
but when he stops listening to the voice and starts listening
to the noise of the storm, he sinks. And Jesus says, "Oh, you
of little faith..."

I get uncomfortable when I recall that passage, because I don't
think that Jesus is really talking to Peter. After all, Peter had
faith; Peter stepped out of the boat! I think Jesus is looking
past Peter, at the *other* disciples in the boat... I think Jesus is
looking at me! I think he is saying, "Oh, you of little faith...
why don't *you* step out of the boat? Why don't you leave
your comfort zone? Why don't you do what you're hesitant
to do? What are you afraid of? Don't you know that I will
save you? Don't you know that you will not perish? Don't
you know that no one can take you out of my Father's hand?"

I don't think I've ever *stepped* out of the boat in my life... but I have been *thrown* out a few times!

I was working at my "dream job" in 1992. I had started with the company back when it was so small that we sometimes had to take money from the coin laundry machines to meet our payroll... and, during my tenure, the firm had grown into a national organization. We were very successful, and I had a big desk in a spacious office that overlooked the heart of downtown. I was pleased and prosperous.

At 8:04 a.m. on my fifteenth anniversary with the company, my office phone rang. My boss wanted to see me. I quickly moved to the elevator, anticipating what I would receive to commemorate my anniversary. A gold watch? A bonus? Maybe a nice paid vacation! But never mind – I'd settle for a handshake and an acknowledgement that I had been a valuable part of their success.

Without even inviting me to sit down, my boss gave me the word: "We've decided to let you go. Be out of here today. And have someone sign for your front door key." To say I was devastated would be an understatement: I hadn't been out of work since I was sixteen years old! In the days and weeks of unemployment that followed, I held on to scripture passages like this one: "You will not perish... I will save you... and no one can take you out of my Father's hand."

One day, during a particularly "down" time, my wife asked me, "What would you do if money was not an issue?" My response was fast and easy: "I'd go back to college, get a religious studies degree, and go to work for the church!" Her response was just as fast: "So do it!" But I had a long list of reasons why I couldn't – we have two kids in college, we need to save for retirement, we can't live on one salary, etc.

Come Next Spring
James R. Welter

My older son's voice boomed from the next room: "Dad, if you're going to walk on water, you have to get out of the boat!"

I went back to college and got that degree, which led to working in a parish... which led to a nationwide reflection ministry... which led to my writing two books... which gave me an opportunity to touch many lives. But most of all, the experience gave me a renewed faith in the words of Jesus: "I will save you. You will not perish. And no one can take you out of my Father's hand."

So... what boat are *you* being invited to step out of today? Is it a destructive relationship? A dead-end job? A stalled career? Maybe it's a compulsive habit, or a loss in your life. Whatever it is, try to hear the promise of Easter. And hear the words of Jesus, spoken to you...

"I will save you. You will not perish. And no one can take you out of my Father's hand!"

Reflection

1. What "boat" in your life do you need to step out of? What is holding you back from making that change?

2. Does the fact that previous difficult situations in your life have turned out well ease your anxiety about your current problems or situation? Why or why not?

3. What would you do with your life if money was not a concern, or did not need to be considered? Why haven't you done so? What is it that keeps you from pursuing your dream?

Do You Love Me?   *John 21:15-17*

When they had finished breakfast, Jesus said to Simon Peter, "Simon, son of John, do you love me more than these?" He said to him, "Yes, Lord, you know that I love you." He said to him, "Feed my lambs." He then said to him a second time, "Simon, son of John, do you love me?" He said to him, "Yes, Lord, you know that I love you." He said to him, "Tend my sheep." He said to him the third time, "Simon, son of John, do you love me?" Peter was distressed that he had said to him a third time, "Do you love me?" and he said to him, "Lord, you know everything; you know that I love you." Jesus said to him, "Feed my sheep.

"What would you really like to do?" My wife's question startled me. "I'd like to find a job," I shot back, without looking up from the want-ads. But she persisted, "If money was not a concern, what would you *really* like to do?" "I'd like to retire," I said, and began my list of "buts": "...but we don't have enough money saved; I'd like to go back to school, but we still have two kids in college. I'd like to work for the church, but they don't pay enough." Just then, our oldest son placed a book on the table in front of me, it was one I had given him as he completed high school. The title screamed at me: "Get Off Your Buts: Leaving Your Comfort Zone."

After much "wailing and gnashing of teeth," I finally left my comfort zone. I didn't get a job; instead, I became a fifty-two-year-old college freshman and my wife financially supported me. I was sure I heard my father turning over in his grave – and my comfort zone was out of sight!

The apostles are way outside their comfort zone in today's reading – they, too, had left their jobs to follow that itinerant preacher, Jesus, for three years... and now he was dead.

So now the apostles have returned to Galilee. They're getting back into their comfort zone by going back to what they know: fishing!

As they row their small boat and haul their nets, the morning sun reveals a strange sight. They strain their eyes: "Is that *Jesus* standing there on the shore?!" Peter, always the impulsive one, puts on his cloak and jumps into the water to get to him. Jesus must have joked with Peter over breakfast later that morning – "Peter, wouldn't it have been better if you had gotten dressed *after* your swim?" But the mood soon changes, as Jesus looks at Peter and asks him a startling question: "Simon, son of John, do you love me?" And not once, but *three times* he asks this! Finally Peter gets upset, and emphatically responds, "Lord, you know all things – you know that I love you!" And then Jesus paints an image of what is to come: "Simon, when you were young, you fastened your belt and went where you pleased. But when you are old, someone will come, you will stretch forth your hands... and they will tie you, and lead you where you do not want to go!"

Many Bible commentaries tell us Peter is asked "Do you love me?" three times, to atone for the three times he denied Jesus. That's a good explanation of the passage, but it leaves the encounter between Jesus and Peter; it doesn't draw *me* in or challenge *me* to leave my comfort zone.

Some scholars believe there is more going on in this passage, and it centers on how we translate the word "love." In our culture, we have one word for "love," and we use it to express all levels of that emotion.

I "love" television, I "love" to read, I "love" my cat, I "love" pizza... I "love" my wife! Wait a minute: how can I use the same word to express my craving for pizza and my relationship with my wife?

The Greeks (one of whom was John, the writer of the fourth gospel) had no such linguistic limitation. They had several words to express love, among them *eros*, *philia*, and *agape*. "Eros" (from which we derive the word "erotic") has to do with the romantic, sensual expression of love. "Philia" is a brotherly camaraderie, a sort of "business partner" kind of love. It is conditional; it says "I will love you as long as you do this, or until you do that." "Agape" expresses a boundless, unconditional love. It is the kind of love that Mother Theresa had for the poor and suffering, or that parents might have for their child; it is the kind of unlimited, unrestricted, unending love that God has for each one of us.

"Simon, son of John, do you 'agape' me?" Jesus asks. But Peter responds in a different tense: "Yes, Lord, I 'philia' you." And so Jesus asks a second time, "Simon, son of John, do you 'agape' me?" And Simon again responds, "Yes, I 'philia' you, Lord." And so a third time, Jesus asks, "Simon, son of John, do you 'agape' me?" Now Peter gets upset: "Lord, you know all things – you know that I have denied you; you know my love is imperfect; you know I am weak... you know I can only 'philia' you!"

Peter is not angry with Jesus; he is angry with *himself*. And Jesus is not simply badgering him with questions; Jesus is asking Peter for a total, wholehearted commitment of love that Peter knows he isn't capable of giving, much as he might want to. And so he is ashamed and upset.

But Jesus tells him, "I tell you, Simon, when you were young, you fastened your belt and went where you pleased. But when you are old, someone will come, you will stretch forth your hands... and they will tie you, and lead you where you would not go." In other words, Jesus isn't so much warning Peter or pronouncing his doom as he is saying, "Don't be upset, Peter; I understand why you can't 'agape' me – you're too

young, too used to doing your own thing, and this sort of commitment is too demanding. You're afraid, and you don't want to do it... it's more than you're capable of giving right now. But when you're older, with more wisdom and maturity, and you've lived long enough to see beyond your own fears and concerns... then you will be able to stretch forth your hands... and others will tie you and take you to that place you don't want to go."

The years pass. The scene changes, and now Peter is an old man. Tradition tells us that one day, while leaving Rome to escape persecution, Peter sees Jesus walking towards him on the road and he says, "*Quo vadis, Domine?*" "Where are you going, Lord?" And Jesus says, "I'm going to Jerusalem to be crucified again." And Peter remembers the words spoken to him so long ago: "When you were young, you fastened your belt and went where you pleased. But when you are old, someone will come, you will stretch forth your hands... and they will tie you, and lead you where you would not go." And Peter realizes that he must do as Jesus would, and return to Rome to be with the Christians who are dying there.

So Peter returns to Rome, and tradition tells us that he is crucified there, upside down. And as he hangs on the cross, he again hears the words of Jesus: "Simon, son of John, do you 'agape' me?" And Peter, gasping for breath, with blood running from his mouth as he gives his very life for his Master, can say at last, "Yes, Lord — I 'agape' you!"

With this understanding of scripture, I can no longer dismiss the passage as an encounter between Jesus and Peter. Instead, I now hear Jesus speaking to *me*. "Jim, son of Joseph, do you 'agape' me? Will you stretch forth your hands and let me lead you to that place you would not go?"

To the extent that we can answer "yes" to that question, he will lead us where we would not go.

He will lead us to suffering. He will lead us to growth. He will lead us to an understanding of love.

He will lead us – to life!

Reflection

1. When has God lead you a place you did not want to go? What were the circumstances? Why were you resistant? How did you learn or grow from that experience?

2. Give an example of a time when you left your "comfort zone." How did you resist? What were your objections to the change? What was the outcome of the experience?

3. Name one thing you would like to do or become before you die. What prevents you from doing it? Why?

4. What might the story of Peter, as presented above, teach us about suffering? Growth? Love? What lessons might we draw from this story as to why we must suffer in life?

The Third Chapter:
In the Garden

Awake, O north wind, and come, O south wind!
Blow upon my garden...
                                    (Song of Solomon 4:15)

The image of a garden is often used in scripture, beginning with the book of Genesis and its story of creation. We are given a beautiful image of our God, who "comes down" and walks in the garden with Adam (who symbolizes all mankind). This image reveals to us the intimate relationship God has with his creation, and it is a precursor to God "coming down" in human form to be one with us.

Every time we witness new life or observe a new season, we see God "in the garden." These experiences remind us that we, too, have been planted and are growing from death into life again. We should not be surprised, then, to find Jesus spending his last night talking with his Father in a garden. And it is fitting, also, that Mary Magdalene should encounter the Risen Lord in a garden.

As on that last night, God is with us in the garden as we suffer our doubts, fear, and pain.

Like that first morning and like that first Easter, God walks with us in the garden and sows the seeds of surprise – the seeds of new life!

Come and See John 1:45-46

Philip found Nathanael and said to him, "We have found him of whom Moses in the Law and also the prophets wrote, Jesus of Nazareth, the son of Joseph." Nathanael said to him, "Can anything good come from Nazareth?" Philip said to him, "Come and see."

"The Bible is the inspired word of God!" the man next to me at the lunch counter suddenly blurted out. I was the only other person at the counter just then, so I had to assume that his statement was directed at me. "Everything is either the truth or a lie, isn't it?" he went on. Without giving me a chance to respond, the man continued: "If Jesus said he was God, then he is either who he said he was... or he's a liar; isn't that right?" He sat back, confident that he had created a classic "false dilemma" which would force me to accept his understanding of Jesus and the scriptures. "Well, let's first discuss what the Bible is, how we understand 'inspiration,' and what we mean by 'truth,'" I responded. "Then, if we can define what you mean by a 'lie,' maybe I can answer your question." He countered with a rapid-fire series of scripture quotes, totally ignoring my comments.

In the scripture passage above, cynical Nathanael scoffs at the suggestion that the Messiah could come from "the ends of the earth" when he says to Philip, "Can anything good come from Nazareth?" But Philip knew what my antagonist did not – that theological argument does not bring people to Jesus. So Philip doesn't try to persuade Nathanael through argument, but instead simply invites him to "Come and see."

I have been involved in the RCIA (Rite of Christian Initiation for Adults) programs of several parishes for more than twenty years, but I have yet to meet anyone who was

drawn to inquire about the church because of some theological argument. No, they always come because of a relationship – because someone has invited them. Someone once advised me, "Don't tell them what you believe; show them how you got there." In other words, invite them to "come and see." Invite them to "walk the parable road" with you.

I recently saw a sticker on the back of a car that said, "Honk if you love Jesus!" And it reaffirmed my feeling that, the more confusing and uncertain the world gets, the more people seem to be attracted to the slogans, rules, rituals, shortcuts, and easy answers of what I call "bumper-sticker" religion – that so-called "spirituality" which says "just rally around my cause, mouth my formulas, follow my rules, adopt my definitions, believe in my answers... and you can have Jesus!"

"Did you believe, just because I said I saw you under a fig tree?" Jesus asks Nathanael. Come and see what it's *really* about! Come and "walk the parable road" with me.

The "parable road" isn't where we trumpet easy answers, it's where we ask the hard questions: "Who is my neighbor?" "When did we see you hungry?" "What must I do?" "Where were you when my sister died?" "Why must good people suffer?" And we *struggle* with the answers. Sometimes we find them... and sometimes we must keep on searching.

It is on this road that you can see my faith lived out; it is on this road that I can share with you the source of my hope and my strength. It is on this road that you can see how I manage to "hold on," and why I keep coming back to the table. It is on the "parable road" that Jesus can be found.

Come and see!

Reflection

1. Nathanael finds Jesus in the most unexpected place, at the "ends of the earth"... in Nazareth! In what unusual place or circumstances have you found Jesus? Why do you believe you found him there?

2. What are some of the unanswered questions in your life? How do you respond to "bumper-sticker" Christians who approach you with their "formulas for salvation" or other pat answers for your life? Do you sometimes encounter this same "bumper-sticker" mentality in your own faith community? (Christian formulas can also be centered around special rituals, prayers, devotions, or dogmas.) How do you respond?

3. Give some examples from the Christian scriptures of people who hold a similar "bumper-sticker" understanding or relationship with God. How does Jesus respond to them?

I Must Stay at Your House   *Luke 19:1-5*

He entered Jericho and was passing through. And
there was a man named Zacchaeus. He was a chief
tax collector and was rich. And he was seeking to
see who Jesus was, but on account of the crowd he
could not, because he was small of stature. So he ran
on ahead and climbed up into a sycamore tree to see
him, for he was about to pass that way. And when
Jesus came to the place, he looked up and said to
him, "Zacchaeus, hurry and come down, for I must
stay at your house today."

I wonder why Jesus chose to stay with Zacchaeus? He
certainly wasn't the only sinner available in the crowd that
day! But he was a *public* sinner – a tax collector. In Jesus'
time, tax collectors were especially despised and were treated
as outcasts, because they collected money for the hated
Roman rulers and were allowed to keep a high percentage for
themselves. Thus, they accumulated great wealth by
collaborating with foreign conquerors at the expense of their
own people. Zacchaeus was a "chief tax collector" and was no
doubt hated by many; maybe he was chosen that day because
his conversion would be more dramatic.

Jesus was a very social person. I don't think he associated
with prostitutes, tax collectors, and sinners merely to seek
their conversion; I think he truly liked those kinds of people.
Yes, they were sinners and outcasts – but they were also
authentic, "real" people. They didn't put on airs or pretend
to be "one of the crowd," and they lived their lives a little
outside the "social norms" of their day, just as Jesus did.

Zacchaeus is a wealthy man and seems to have a good sense
of who he is; he doesn't let the label "tax collector" define or
limit him. And he doesn't care what the neighbors think:

while dressed in his finest clothes, he climbs a tree in public because he wants to see this "Jesus" he's heard so much about!

Jesus doesn't let the label "messiah" – and what people think *that* means – define him, either. And he doesn't care what the neighbors think: he embraces Zacchaeus, this well-known sinner, as a friend, and goes with him to his house for dinner.

No wonder these two hit it off! They have a lot in common, and spending the day together would be fun. Both have the strength to be themselves – to be genuine, to be authentic, to be "real." Neither allows his actions to be dictated by "shoulds" and "oughts," or by the judgment or approval of those around them. Both know who they are, and their sense of self doesn't depend on what others say about them.

As Christians, we somtimes speak of the "real presence" of Jesus in the Eucharist. It makes for interesting theological discussion to ask exactly what that means, and to struggle with the idea as we try to define the indefinable. But the more important question is: how are *we* the "real presence" of Jesus in our world? How are we "real" and "present" to each other? Are we genuine and authentic in our relationships? Are we confident enough to "do our own thing" in living our faith? Or do we compromise ourselves and allow social norms, societal values, and the expectations of others to define who we are?

Jesus sees *us* in the trees we climb and says to us, "Come down; I must stay at your house today." He wants to eat with a sinner today.

He wants to eat with *us*!

Will you invite him in?

111

Reflection

1. In what ways do we let society define or label us? What labels does society put on us because of our gender, race, age, or other personal characteristics? How can we work to overcome those labels?

2. Name some "shoulds" and "oughts" that affect your life. How has your life been affected by the expectations of others? What have you done (or what can you do) to move beyond those expectations?

3. When we allow others to label us, we give them power over us. What labels do you think others use to define you? What labels do you assign to yourself? How can you work to remove these labels? Or should you?

4. What sorts of things can we do to rid ourselves of defining labels? To stop labeling others?

Do You See This Woman?   Luke 7:36—39

*One of the Pharisees asked him to eat with him, and he
went into the Pharisee's house and took his place at the
table. And behold, a woman of the city, who was a sinner,
when she learned that he was reclining at table in the
Pharisee's house, brought an alabaster flask of ointment,
and standing behind him at his feet, weeping, she began
to wet his feet with her tears and wiped them with the
hair of her head and kissed his feet and anointed them
with the ointment. Now when the Pharisee who had
invited him saw this, he said to himself, "If this man were
a prophet, he would have known who and what sort of
woman this is who is touching him, for she is a sinner."*

There is a classic *koan* (or "teaching riddle") in Buddhism in
which the master asks the student, "Is the white horse
white?" The student quickly responds with the obvious
answer, "Yes." And the master asks again, "Is the white horse
white?" Again the student answers, this time with a little
irritation, "Yes." For a third time, the master asks the student,
"Is the white horse white?" And now the student begins to
understand: white is the *color* of the horse, not what the
horse *is* – and to really *see* the horse, we must see *past* its
color.

In the scripture passage above, Jesus is reclining at dinner as
a guest at Simon's house when a woman comes in and begins
to bathe his feet with ointment and her tears. Simon, an
upright Pharisee, is appalled that Jesus would let a known
sinner touch him, much less bathe his feet! And so Jesus
asks him, "Simon, do you see this woman?"

Jesus knows that Simon doesn't "see" the woman; all he
sees is a sinner. Then Jesus says, "Simon, let me tell you
a story: two people were in debt to a certain creditor; one
owed five hundred days' wages and the other owed fifty.

Since neither was able to repay the debt, he forgave it for both of them. Simon, in this situation, who do you think loved him the most?" And Simon said in reply, "I suppose it was the one who was forgiven the most."

Simon is like a kid in school who guesses at a true-or-false question; he gives the right answer, but he doesn't know *why* it's right. So Jesus says, "I'm going to tell you why you're right. Simon, do you see this woman? When I came to your house, you gave me no water for my feet, but she is washing my feet with her tears. You gave me no kiss of greeting, but she has not stopped kissing my feet. You gave me no oil for my beard, while she covers me with perfume. Simon, do you *see* this woman? She loves much because she has been forgiven much!"

It was a beautiful summer day in South Haven, Michigan – the sun was shining and there wasn't a cloud in the sky. It was the first day of our vacation, and the sign at the bed-and-breakfast said we were only "one hundred steps from the beach." "Let's go!" I called to my wife, anxious to get the day started. "Oh, honey," – there was a hint of panic in her voice – "we didn't bring any beach towels!" And I was at my problem-solving best: "Look, there's a shop called 'Sand and Surf' right across the street; I'll bet they have beach towels!" "They'll be too expensive there," she replied, "I saw a Wal-Mart on the way into town; let's go there instead." I sighed. From long experience, I knew logic was useless in situations like this; my best bet was to make the trip as quickly as possible. I didn't know what the speed limits were in South Haven, but I'm sure I broke them all getting us to our destination! As we entered Wal-Mart, I sprinted into the lead, grabbed two beach towels, and headed for the express checkout lane. "Honey," I heard my wife say – and the tone was all too familiar – "they're on *sale* at this table!"

A hook shot sent the overpriced towels back to the rack they came from as I lunged for the discount table. "Look!" – and again, that tone which causes shopaholics from aisles around to come running – "they have bathing suits on sale too!" It was all over. I was defeated and I knew it. My wife had entered "bargain hunting" mode, and I was firmly convinced that we would spend this sunny day, if not our entire vacation, in Wal-Mart! I was fuming, but I managed a reasonably civil response: "Honey, I noticed that there's a McDonalds here in the store; I'll just go have a cup of coffee while you shop." And so I did.

In the restaurant, however, I ended up standing behind an overweight woman who couldn't seem to make up her mind about what to order. By this time, I was getting a headache and my patience was long since exhausted. "C'mon, move it, lady!" I grumbled to myself. "If I can't spend the day at the beach, at least let me get a cup of coffee! What's taking you so long?" At last, after much delay, she finally ordered a milkshake. "Geez, lady," I mocked silently, "why not order a salad? You need a milkshake like you need a hole in the head!"

With my coffee in hand, I turned to find a table – and there, right in front of me, sitting in wheelchairs, were four of the most severely deformed young men I have ever seen. Their bodies were twisted, their speech was loud and slurred, and drool ran down their chins. "There's a table in the corner," I instantly thought, "I'll just go over there..." Instead, I stopped myself. Overcome with shame, I forced myself to sit nearby. Trying to at least look at the crippled young men, I struggled silently to pray: "Father, have mercy on..."

Just then, the overweight woman came over to them, and with her napkin, she gently wiped the drool from the face of the first young man and began feeding him her milkshake.

115

I heard the challenge of the Buddha that day: "Is the white horse white?"

And I also heard the words of Jesus: "Jim, do you see this woman? The one you mocked and were so quick to judge? You sought to avoid those boys, but she sits next to them. You can barely force yourself to look at them, but she gives them her full attention. You struggle even to pray for them, but she has not ceased wiping their faces and satisfying their thirst. Do you *see* this woman?"

My wife's voice brought me back to reality: "Honey, I'm ready now!" she called, as she moved toward the checkout lane.

As I left the coffee shop, I again heard the voice of Jesus.

"Jim! In this situation... who do you think loved the most?"

Reflection

1. Share an incident from your life in which you were challenged by the gospel. How did you respond to that challenge?

2. Tell about a time when you misjudged another person, or made assumptions about them based on your own prejudices or misconceptions. How did you feel when you discovered you were in error? How did the experience change your life or your attitude?

3. Although the story of the white horse comes from the Buddhist tradition, it certainly ties in very strongly with the gospel message. What other wisdom from different cultures do you see being reflected in, or showing a strong connection with, the gospels?

4. What person or circumstance has helped you to "see" people as Jesus "sees" them? What can you do to remind yourself to continue "seeing" people this way in the future?

Teach Us to Pray   Luke 11:1-3

Now Jesus was praying in a certain place, and when he finished, one of his disciples said to him, "Lord, teach us to pray, as John taught his disciples." And he said to them, "This is how you are to pray: Our Father in heaven, hallowed be thy name, thy kingdom come, thy will be done on earth as in heaven. Give us this day our daily bread..."

There was a priest in the 1950s who launched a nationwide prayer campaign with the slogan, "The family that prays together stays together." Our family signed on. I was ten years old, and my father had already been in the state hospital in Logansport, Indiana, for five years. And so we prayed each night, believing that this would surely be the prayer that would bring Papa home. Summer tuned to winter, and winter into spring. Year followed year; children became adults. Our prayers never stopped. And my father never came home. After twenty-five years, he died in that institution.

I know people who insist that all you have to do to sell real estate is to bury a statue of St. Joseph. I've heard testimonies from people who claim to have prayed and had cancers taken away. Others tell of committing their life to Christ and having their careers turned around, or their failing businesses saved. I'm happy for them if that's their experience. But it hasn't been mine. I'm in the back pew and I want to scream, "I prayed and my father never came home! I prayed and my sister died of cancer! I'm committed to Christ and I still lost my job!"

I suspect it is from experiences such as these that the apostles approached Jesus one day and asked, "Lord, teach us to pray." As Jews, the apostles obviously knew "how" to pray – they knew the words, they had been taught the formulas, and they

had no doubt heard miraculous success stories. Yet they must have felt that something wasn't working for them. So they approached Jesus and wanted to know how to "do it right." And Jesus' answer to them was the "Our Father."

I doubt it was the answer that the apostles were expecting.

I wonder where Jesus got that prayer? A careful reading of the text leads me to believe that it didn't drop out of the sky – rather, I think it was born out of his life experience. One can almost see the influence of Mary and Joseph in this prayer; who better to teach Jesus "thy will be done," than the one whose answer to God was "let it be done according to your word"? And who better to teach him "give us this day our daily bread," than the one who left his job, uprooted his family, and moved to Egypt in the middle of the night, trusting in God to provide?

In scripture, Jesus always prays "in the now." He prays humbly and simply, from his life experience.

And he doesn't make extravagant requests – he prays for what he needs "this day." He prays before he eats, he prays during temptation, he prays before major decisions, and he prays when he is fearful and in doubt. And he teaches us to pray from our life experience too. Sometimes we pray in a whisper, sometimes in song; sometimes our prayer is a scream. It may begin with a plea – "let this cup pass" – but it must always end in acceptance: "thy will be done!"

"Thy will be done" – that's the tough part. That's the "faith" part. That's the "letting go" part. That's the part that gives us trouble, just as it probably did for the apostles. Because that's when we realize we can't manipulate God by saying the right words, burying statutes, counting prayer beads, or

following formulas. That's when we realize that prayer really shouldn't be about what *we* want – but about what *he* wants. That's when we realize we shouldn't pray in order to change God's mind... we should pray in order to change our hearts.

May we pray from our life experience, and may our prayer be the song we sing: "Lord! This time... change our hearts."

Reflection

1. Most of our prayers are petitions or "to-do" lists for God. We say things like: "Find me a job. Cure my illness. Keep our children safe. Make me successful. Send us more priests," etc. What is "wrong" with this type of prayer?

2. There are seven petitions in the Lord's Prayer. What are they? How do these petitions differ from the ones we usually mention in prayer?

3. What does how we pray say about our relationship with God?

4. When we pray to "win" (a game, a promotion, etc.), we are, in effect, praying for someone else to "lose." What does this reveal about our prayer life, or our understanding of God? How might we work toward changing these attitudes?

5. If our prayers can change God's mind, it means that, in a sense, we have power over God. Is this really what is meant by "the power of prayer"? If not, what else could it mean?

Labels   *John 9:1-2*

As he passed by he saw a man blind from birth. His disciples asked him, "Rabbi, who sinned, this man or his parents, that he was born blind?"

"And be sure to put a label on each jar!" It was my oldest sister, Dot, giving final instructions to the workforce of younger siblings who were taking part in the annual canning process on our farm, back in the 1950s. (It was never clear to us younger siblings why the process was called "canning" when we always used glass jars!)

A ladder lowered through a trapdoor in the bedroom closet led to the cellar, where canned goods were stored. The "cellar" was really only a hole my father had dug under the house, but its dirt walls, lined with wooden shelves, provided a cool place for food in the summer and prevented our provisions from freezing in the winter.

In the darkness of the cellar, the dim light of a kerosene lantern made it difficult to distinguish beans from peas, or apples from peaches. "We need labels so we know what's in the jars," Dot would explain, in an effort to keep the production line moving.

We all love to label things. Labeling gives us an element of order and control: we always want to know "what's in the jars," so we label files and cartons, date our photographs, and include subject lines in our e-mails. This practice simplifies our understanding and makes life easier.

Let's put ourselves into this story from the gospel of John: Jesus and his followers (that's us) come upon a man who has been blind since birth. We immediately label him a sinner and we ask, "Lord, whose sin caused this man to be

born blind – his own, or that of his parents?" The label we have placed on this man blinds *us* to all other possibilities. Never mind that this person is a beggar in need of help. Never mind that he has spent his entire life in the "dark cave" of blindness. Never mind that this person sits within earshot of our voice and can hear what we are saying. Forget all that – let's talk about his sin, so we can get him labeled and categorized and under control... so we don't have to think about him any further.

Labeling is the easy road; labeling gets us off the hook. It's easier to label a person's problems than it is to help the person with them. Placing labels is so easy; it requires no effort on our part... and then we can stop thinking about the label's recipient!

It's easier to label than it is to listen. It's easier to label than it is to love.

When we apply labels to people, we assume that there is only one thing in the "jar." We assume that the only thing in the jar is what *we* can see in the faint light of our kerosene lantern! In the dim cellar of our limited experience, and in the darkness of our "shoulds" and "oughts," we place our labels on all those of whom we do not approve... on all those whom we do not understand... on all those who are different from us.

"Be careful what you label" – Dot never seemed to run out of instructions! – "because once you put the label on, it's hard to get it off!"

And the most difficult labels to remove are those that we place on *ourselves*. We subtly apply those "self labels" every time we say "I am a...," rather than, "I am a person who..." Those are often the labels that stick the most firmly.

Those are the labels that limit our vision and disguise our gifts. Placing labels is so easy. It requires no effort... and then we can stop thinking!

It's easier to label than to learn. It's easier to label than to discover. It's easier to label than to grow.

"Teacher," we might ask Jesus, "whose label caused *this* person to be blind?"

Reflection

1. What labels do we as individuals, and as a society, put on people? Why do we so readily label people?

2. What label has often been put on you? How has this label limited your freedom? Your understanding of yourself?

3. Finish this sentence: " I am a(n) _____, and _____, and _____." How do these labels limit your freedom, self-development, or growth?

4. What labels in your life would you like to remove from yourself or others? What changes would doing this entail?

Buried Talents　　　　　　　Luke 19: 20-22

Then another came, saying, "Lord, here is your money, which I kept laid away in a handkerchief; for I was afraid of you, because you are a severe man. You take what you did not deposit, and reap what you did not sow." He said to him, "I will condemn you with your own words, you wicked servant! You knew that I was a severe man, taking what I did not deposit and reaping what I did not sow?"

The word "parable" comes from the Greek word *parabolein*. That word has two parts: *para*, meaning *beside,* and *bolein,* meaning *to throw.* So the word *parable* may be interpreted as that which we *throw (or place) beside.* In other words, the listener or reader is asked to place the story beside his or her life experience and compare the two to see what lessons can be learned.

"Which one of you..." are the words Jesus often uses to begin his parables and draw the listeners into the story. By definition, parables are open-ended – they have no defined interpretation or conclusion; the listener finishes the story on their own, from their own experience. And Jesus invites us to take that step when he asks questions such as "Who do you think was the neighbor?" (Luke 10:36).

The parable of the talents, which appears in Luke's gospel, is a little strange; it sounds more like a lesson in fiscal planning than a parable! In the story, the king goes away and leaves his servants with his money, to use as they think best while he is gone. Although there are no strings attached, this is obviously a test to see if the king's subjects will be prudent and faithful in the use of the money entrusted to them. Upon his return, the king rewards those who used the money and punishes the one who buried it for safekeeping.

We usually interpret this story to mean that we must not bury the gifts and talents God gives us, but should instead use them for God's glory and the coming of his kingdom.

That's a good and valuable lesson, but it's not the only one to be learned from this story – and it's not the one I hear today as I place this passage beside my own life experience. I find myself identifying with the man who buried his treasure! I identify with the man who says, in effect, "I'm not going to play your game!" I'm not going to be entrapped in your world of competition; I don't believe that winning is "the only thing" and that the one in second place is the "first loser." I don't get my value as a person from multiplying your money – I don't equate success with making all the bucks I can! And yes, I know you will punish me for not playing by your rules and not accepting your values. But I will not value a person based on what they produce, and I won't empower such behavior in you! That's who I am; that's *my* treasure! I'll use my gifts and talents in ways that reflect who I am, and in the ways I feel the spirit is leading me. That use will reflect *my* values and the statement *I* choose to make to the world!

In parish work, you get invited into a lot of lives and you get to hear a lot of people's stories. I know of many couples that have decided to live on one income so they can be there to raise their children, and I know several "Mr. Moms" who stay home with the kids because that's simply what they do best. I know of a couple that went to adopt one child and came home with *four* – because they didn't want to break up a group of siblings. I know of several other people who have made drastic career changes because they realized that "even if you win the rat race, you're still a rat" – and they wanted more than that from life!

We are expected to use our gifts and talents in ways that will help us become our highest and best selves. When we are true to ourselves, we become whole. And in our wholeness, we become holy – and give glory to God!

Reflection

1. What is your reaction to the author's interpretation of this parable? Do you believe this interpretation is a valuable one? What lessons can you learn from it?

2. What areas of your life are dominated by competition, the expectations of others, or the demands of society? In what ways do these influences conflict with aspects of your life as a Christian? How can (or do) you resolve these conflicts when they arise?

3. What does the phrase "When we are true to ourselves, we become whole" mean to you? How does it relate to the gospel message?

Come Next Spring

How's Your Love Life?   Matthew 25:34-36

Then the King will say to those on his right, "Come, you who are blessed by my Father, inherit the kingdom prepared for you from the foundation of the world. For I was hungry and you gave me food, I was thirsty and you gave me drink, I was a stranger and you welcomed me, I was naked and you clothed me, I was sick and you visited me, I was in prison and you came to me."

It must be one of those "Mars/Venus" things I've read about: when we call our son who lives out of state, my first question is usually, "How's work?" It's a guy thing – work is a safe place where we feel we have some control and expertise. But when I hand the phone to my wife, her "Venus" voice asks him, "How's your love life?" She knows (because she has that female chromosome which holds 90% of all of the world's knowledge!) that the rest of life flows from this question. And Jesus knows it too. In this scripture passage, Matthew reminds us that the only question the Lord will ask when we stand before him is: "How did you treat the least of my brothers and sisters?" In other words, "How was your love life?" How did you treat your neighbor? In short: how did you love?

Oh, we try to complicate it: we make rules and laws; we develop rituals, prayers, and formulas; we create churches and clubs, dues and memberships. We create all sorts of "hoops" for people to jump through so they can enter the kingdom! Of course, rituals are important – they are a part of every religion, age, culture, and family. They connect us to our past and connect us to a group; they give us part of our identity. But we must remember that rituals are a *human* need – they are for *our* benefit. God doesn't need them!

126

We may want someone to be a Catholic or a Christian, to attend church every Sunday, to experience our rituals and express their faith in the same way that we express ours... but that, too, is *our* need — it's not necessarily *God's* need! In fact, Matthew reminds us that Jesus won't even *ask* about those things! Instead, Jesus will ask the "Venus" question: "How's your love life?" How did you love?

Notice that he doesn't ask if we were immersed or sprinkled, if we were Protestant or Catholic, or how often we went to church — or even if we went at all. No, the only question asked is: "How did you love?" Did you feed me when I was hungry? Did you clothe me when I was naked? Did you visit me when I was in prison?

Jesus makes it clear that *anyone* can qualify to enter God's kingdom! You can be a thief on a cross or a doubting Thomas; a prostitute, a tax collector, a leper, or a sinner — it doesn't matter. The only question asked — the sole criteria for judgment — is "How did you treat the least of your brothers and sisters?" In other words, "How did you love?"

But surely, we want to say, not just *anyone* can enter the kingdom! Surely not non-Christians, agnostics, or non-believers! How could that be? They're unsaved! They're sinners! When did they ever serve the Lord?

And these people, too, will ask the question: "When did we see you hungry and feed you, Lord? Or thirsty, and give you drink? When did *we* do your will — we, who know nothing about you, or have never heard of you, or doubt your very existence?"

"When you did it for the least of my brothers and sisters, you did it for me," says the Lord.

127

You answered my call though you knew not my voice; you did my will though you knew not my words... you followed my path though you knew not my name! You did these things whenever you reached out to someone in need – when you fed the hungry or cared for the sick, when you listened, when you comforted, when you helped... when you loved.

Matthew's judgment scene makes it clear that the life we lead speaks louder to God than any formula, words, or rituals we can conceive. It is in the life we lead that we say "yes" to God – and we can say "yes" even while we are questioning, even when we doubt, even as we struggle. Our "yes" to God puts us in touch with Jesus, even though we may not express the connection in that particular way. Yet Jesus makes it very clear that those who do the will of his Father are his brothers and sisters (Matt. 12:50). We may not perform the rituals, we may not know the words... yet by our love and caring for others, we choose Jesus.

"How did you love?"

It's the only question God will ask.

It's the only answer that will matter.

Reflection

1. So, how *do* you love? When was the last time you took a personal interest in someone less fortunate than you? When have you touched the hand or looked into the eyes of the person you were helping? When have you taken the time to listen to their story? If it hasn't been recently, what can you do to remedy that situation?

2. Why do you think that "those on his right" were surprised when Jesus said they were the ones who fed him, clothed him, and visited him? Why might they not have realized what they were doing?

3. Has there ever been a time or occasion in which you think *you* may have done God's will without realizing it? What do you think that says about the ways in which God operates in our lives?

Duct Tape   Mark 9:30-34

They went on from there and passed through Galilee. And he did not want anyone to know, for he was teaching his disciples, saying to them, "The Son of Man is going to be delivered into the hands of men, and they will kill him. And when he is killed, after three days he will rise." But they did not understand the saying, and were afraid to ask him. And they came to Capernaum. And when he was in the house he asked them, "What were you discussing on the way?" But they kept silent, for on the way they had argued with one another about who was the greatest.

(In 2002, a deranged person began randomly mailing envelopes of anthrax to people in the Washington D.C. area. It created a national fear that terrorists might launch biological attacks. The government issued guidelines for people to protect themselves, in which it was suggested that everyone keep an emergency supply of duct tape, plastic sheeting, and bottled water on hand. If an attack came, we were to go into our bathroom and seal the doors and windows with duct tape and plastic. For those who lived through the Cold War in the 1950s and 60s, it was reminiscent of learning in school to crawl under your desk in the event of a nuclear attack.)

"Honey, I'm going to the store – should I buy some duct tape?" My wife replied, "If you can find it on sale." "I'll probably die in the hardware section of Wal-Mart," I mumbled to myself, "and I'll never be found, because nobody will ever think to look for me, an accountant, in the hardware section!"

Back in the 1960s, the threat of nuclear annihilation loomed large, in the form of missile launchers in Cuba and a hostile Russian dictator banging his shoe on the U.N. podium and screaming, "We will bury you!" Personal bomb shelters were the rage back then... my feeling this time is that at least duct tape is cheaper, and if no one sets off a biological weapon, you

can always use it to seal packages. Today's modern-day threat is another reminder that the world is a dangerous place – but then again, the world has *always* been a dangerous place. (Think Mongol hordes, barbarian invaders, or the *blitzkrieg*.) As my brother, Harold, often says, "I don't think we'll get out of this world alive!"

The Psalmist repeatedly says "trust in the Lord" (Ps 37:3) – yet in this gospel passage, Jesus predicts his own suffering and death! (Obviously, trusting in the Lord won't necessarily deliver us from these things.) Jesus' prediction of his own death didn't make much sense to the disciples. It didn't fit with their understanding of what a Messiah was all about, and they were "afraid to question him." In this, the disciples resembled someone who receives an unpleasant diagnosis from the doctor, and refuses to ask any further questions – they just don't want to know. The disciples couldn't grasp the enormity of the death of the Messiah, anyway, so we see them going on with life (albeit bickering about who was the greatest). Maybe there's a message in that for us: go on with life!

The famous writer C.S. Lewis was an atheist who later became a Christian. He was wounded in World War I, lived in England during World War II, and lived on into the Cold War era. Lewis saw war, weapons of mass destruction, and a world in chaos firsthand and close up. And he wrote, "It is perfectly ridiculous to go about whimpering and drawing long faces because the scientists have added one more chance of painful and premature death to a world which already bristles with such chances and in which death itself is not a chance, but a certainty. Let that bomb, when it comes, find us doing sensible and human things – praying, working, teaching, listening to music, bathing the children, playing tennis, chatting to our friends over a pint and a game of darts – not huddled together

like frightened sheep and thinking about bombs. They may break our bodies, but they need not dominate our minds."

Similarly, when Bishop Fulton J. Sheen was 79 years old and waiting to have open-heart surgery, a reporter asked him, "Bishop Sheen, are you afraid to die?" "If I die," the Bishop replied, "Jesus is there. And if I live – Jesus is there."

"Trust in the Lord." Now *that's* good advice.

Maybe we should use that duct tape to seal care packages for the needy, or presents for our friends.

Reflection

1. C.S. Lewis said, "Death is not a chance but a certainty." How does this fact change how you live your life?

2. Do you think that amassing possessions is a subtle way we use to deny the reality of death? Why or why not?

3. In what ways has the threat of a terrorist attack affected your life?

4. What are the positive impacts of terrorist threats? Are there any?

5. How has the reality of the terrorist threat affected your faith?

A Burning Hut   *Luke 6:12-16*

In these days he went out to the mountain to pray, and all night he continued in prayer to God. And when day came, he called his disciples and chose from them twelve, whom he named apostles: Simon, whom he named Peter, and Andrew his brother, and James and John, and Philip, and Bartholomew, and Matthew, and Thomas, and James the son of Alphaeus, and Simon who was called the Zealot, and Judas the son of James, and Judas Iscariot, who became a traitor.

A dark night; a storm at sea. A ship goes down. A lone survivor is washed ashore on a deserted island. The years pass, but the man's prayers for rescue go unanswered as he struggles to survive. He builds a small hut to protect himself from the elements and to store his meager belongings. One night, lightning strikes the hut and it burns to the ground. In despair, the man screams at God: "Haven't I suffered enough? Bad enough that I'm stranded here and you ignore my pleas for help – but now you take what little I have left?!" The next day, a ship lands on the island. "How did you know I was here?" the rescued man asks in disbelief. "We saw your signal fire," the ship's captain replies.

One of the characteristics of Luke's gospel is his portrayal of Jesus as a man of prayer. Before any major event in Luke's gospel, we encounter Jesus praying. So in this gospel passage, just before he chooses his apostles, Luke tells us that Jesus spent the night in prayer.

I wonder what Jesus prayed for that night? If he prayed like we do, he was pretty specific: "Hey God, just send me twelve good men! That's not too much to ask; after all, I'm doing your work!" So, after praying all night, Jesus is sent a group of ambitious, violent, dishonest, doubting, traitorous men from

which to choose his followers! How's that for the answer to a prayer?! And Jesus seems to have wondered about that himself: "How long must I put up with you?" he says to them in one passage. And in another, to Simon Peter, he says, "Get behind me, Satan!" And finally, at the Last Supper: "One of you will betray me."

Like Jesus, we pray for good things: steady employment, someone to love us, healthy kids, success... twelve good men. Scripture assures us that our prayers are always answered – but sometimes that answer isn't very apparent to us. Sometimes all we see is our hut burning! The good news, however, is that God is on our side! He doesn't send people to betray us, or hurt us, or take our job; nor does he send sickness or misfortune to bring us down. Those things all come from decisions and choices that *people* make, and from the fact that, in an imperfect world, bad things sometimes happen. God doesn't burn down the hut – God provides the light.

Like Jesus, we struggle with the "letting go" part of prayer. In the garden, Jesus begins his prayer in a directive tone: "Take this cup from me." Only later does he move on to "Your will be done." Jesus gives testimony that the purpose of prayer is not to change God's mind – it is to change our hearts. I remember a Baptist preacher once saying that, "we shouldn't pray for things God is not likely to give." That is, we shouldn't pray for miraculous cures, freedom from pain, or material success; scripture doesn't promise us any of those things. Rather, we should pray for those things God *does* promise to give us: love, courage, faith, strength, wisdom, comfort, and hope. If we seek his face – if we have the courage to ask, "Where is God in all of this?" – then we can believe that the fires in our lives may light our way to new blessings.

Or, as Paul says, "All things work together for the good, for those that love the Lord." (Romans 8:28)

Try to remember that the next time your hut burns!

Reflection

1. Think of a time when your "hut burned" – when something that you considered bad at the time turned out to be a good thing for you. Do you think God might have been trying to tell you something through that incident? If so, what?

2. Explain the phrase "God doesn't burn the hut – God provides the light." What does it mean? Is this just a "feel-good" platitude, or is it something you really believe?

3. Throughout his gospel, Luke portrays Jesus as a man of prayer. List some examples in scripture of Jesus praying. What were the circumstances of his prayers? What do you think he prayed for in those situations?

4. Give some examples when the prayers of Jesus seemed not to be answered in the way that he asked. What can we learn from these examples?

5. In general, what lessons can we learn from the examples of Jesus at prayer?

The Deal   Matthew 11:20-22

Then he began to denounce the cities where most of his mighty works had been done, because they did not repent. "Woe to you, Chorazin! Woe to you, Bethsaida! For if the mighty works done in you had been done in Tyre and Sidon, they would have repented long ago in sackcloth and ashes. But I tell you, it will be more bearable on the day of judgment for Tyre and Sidon than for you."

It's all about "connecting," my friend says again and again as his frustration grows. "They once again missed an opportunity to connect the (homily, liturgy, presentation) with everyday life!"

I think this is the frustration Jesus is feeling in the passage above. The deeds he performed in Chorazin and Bethsaida were so spectacular that (the passage goes on to say) they would have saved even Sodom from destruction! Still, the people didn't "make the connection." They didn't identify those deeds with the person of Jesus. They just didn't "get it"!

Being connected is the deepest longing of the human heart. We yearn for at least one person who understands us and knows what we are "all about" – one person who is "on the same page" with us. Jesus is angry and frustrated in this passage: he thought that, after all he had done, the people would surely have made the connection! But no, they just don't get it. In fact, *no one* gets it! He must have smiled wearily and thought to himself, "At one point, Peter *almost* had it! In the shade of that olive tree, when the big lug shouted, 'You are the Christ!' (Mt 16:16) – in that brief, shining moment, I thought there was a connection; I thought someone at last understood!"

Like us, the apostles thought they had "made the connection" with Jesus. They thought they understood the mission they were on and what was going to happen. But Jesus knew they were at the "deal-making," "bargain-hunting" stage of their faith journey. Their low level of faith is revealed every time Jesus speaks of his suffering and death: they either ignore it or want to change the subject. "Don't talk like that, Jesus," they protest. "Messiahs don't suffer. You're not going to die; (Mt 16:22) you're going to bring about the kingdom and lead us all to glory!'"

They are so excited that the Messiah has finally come! They promise everything: "Master, I'll follow you wherever you go!" (Mt 8:19). And Jesus tries to warn them: you're not connecting! You don't get it! "Foxes have dens, and birds have nests, but the Son of Man has no place to lay his head!" (Mt 8:20). Oh Jesus, they protest – we get it! We know what the deal is: we might be inconvenienced; we may miss a meal or two, or have to sleep without a pillow for a few nights. We might even be homeless for a while. But that's a small price to pay on the road to glory!

Although I wasn't conscious of it at the time, I made a bargain with God early in my life. I made the same deal that the older brother had in the story of the Prodigal Son. In effect, I said: "I'll do everything I'm 'supposed' to do – I'll stay home and work the farm, and I'll be faithful and love as best I can. I'll be an honest person, take care of my family, and go to church regularly. That's my part. In return, I expect you, God, to look out for me... and maybe throw a little miracle or a few blessings my way from time to time."

That's the deal!

Like the disciples, we stand with Jesus and promise, "I will follow you wherever you go." But our "deal" with God is

quickly unmasked when something bad happens to us. It is unmasked whenever our security is threatened, or sickness comes, or a loved one dies. It is unmasked when misfortune strikes, when we lose our job, or when a relationship fails. Over time, life pushes us until our "deal" with God is exposed and the "conditions" we have placed on our faith are laid bare – and we shout, "Where are you, God, in my time of need?"

We begin to truly connect with Jesus when we can admit to ourselves that it was *our* "deal," not God's! We begin to connect when we realize that we cannot dictate terms to God. We begin to connect with Jesus when we at last come to realize that our vision is too limited, and our idea of God is too small.

It's Sunday morning, and I'm attending my first Mass as Business Manager at St. Monica's Parish. The pastor, Fr. Clem Davis, is preaching the homily on the 25th Anniversary of his ordination. I'm not listening; I'm busy trying to figure out how I'm going to make ends meet on a church salary. I'm thinking, "I'll cut back on my contributions to the church. After all, I'm working for less than half of what I was making in the corporate world – what more does God want from me?"

Just then, I hear Fr. Clem proclaim in a loud voice: "God has no hidden agenda – he wants it *all!*"

That's the deal.

Reflection

1. What "deal" or bargain have you made with God?   What does your answer say about your faith and belief system?

2. Is the way you live out your faith still determined by this understanding of your relationship with God?

3. Has your "bargain" with God changed?   What event or experience caused you to rethink your relationship with God?

4. In recognizing your "deal" with God, what concepts or beliefs did you have to re-think, discard, or let go of?

Look At These Stones   **Luke 21:5-6**

While some people were speaking about how the temple was adorned with costly stones and votive offerings, he said, "All that you see here – the days will come when there will not be one stone left standing on another."

One of Ronald Reagan's favorite speeches was entitled "A Shining City on a Hill." I heard him deliver it twice before he was president and several times thereafter. It was a spellbinding speech about his vision of the future of mankind, in which he sees America as "a shining city on a hill." The image for that speech was taken from the book of Revelation. And no doubt the New Testament city of Jerusalem was the source of the imagery: the shining city sitting on a hill, with the temple – the most magnificent structure of its day – glistening in the sun.

This is the scene that Jesus and the apostles saw as they approached Jerusalem one day. The followers of Jesus were simple fishermen – "country bumpkins" by urban standards. They looked at the city from afar, and were very impressed. As they approached the city, they were still wide-eyed! Peter, as he gazed in awe at the Temple, said, "Lord, look at those stones!" I envision Jesus putting his arm around Peter and saying, "Oh, Peter – you're so easily impressed!" "Well, aren't *you*? Look at the size of these stones!" "Peter, do you want to hear something really impressive? The day will come when not one of these stones will be left standing on another!" "Teacher, you really know how to put a damper on things! Here we are – we haven't been to town in months, and we're enjoying a tour of downtown Jerusalem – and then you go and say something like that! Why are you telling me this?" "Because, Peter, I want you to put your trust in something that will never crumble. I want you to put your faith in that which is everlasting!"

We, too, are impressed with "things." Like Peter, we are impressed with the size of the "stones."

Do you know how much money I made last year? Lord, look at these stones!

Did you know that I'm the president of my company? Lord, look at these stones!

Have you seen my nice suits, my lake cottage, my shiny new SUV? Lord, look at these stones!

If we learn the lessons that Jesus would teach us, the stones in our lives will become as rubble at our feet.

We will realize that all material things pass away. And we will be able to say at last: "Lord, look at these stones." The ones I built, the ones I trusted, the ones I put my confidence in – you have allowed to fall. The stones of selfishness, the stones of prejudice, the ones I would cast at my neighbor – you have asked me to lay down. The stones that have been stumbling blocks to me, the ones that have caused me to fear and falter – you have rolled away.

Lord, look at these stones!

Reflection

1. On what "things" do you depend to make you feel safe? What "stones" have you put your trust in?

2. Name one stone or element of security in your life that has collapsed. Was it something you voluntarily let go of, or was it taken from you?

3. In what way have you grown from the experience?

In The Garden   John 20:15

"Jesus said to her, "Woman, why are you weeping? Whom are you looking for?" She thought it was the gardener...

"They're plowing the garden!"

Mom's comment at breakfast echoed one of the first signs of Spring on the farm in Northern Indiana where I grew up. The sound of a tractor plowing the garden meant we had survived another winter and things would be better now. Soon the orchard would be alive with the scent of apple blossoms and their fruit would burst forth and be ours for the taking. Mulberries on the tree would be a precursor of blackberries on the vine, and spring rains would cause the mushrooms to sprout.

In scripture, the image of a garden symbolizes an intimate relationship with God. The story of our relationship with God begins and ends in a garden! It begins in the book of Genesis with the story of creation. We are given a beautiful image of God, who "comes down" and walks in the garden with Adam. It reveals to us the intimate relationship God has with his creation, and it is a precursor to God "coming down" in human form to be one with us.

So, it isn't surprising to see Jesus spend his last night talking with his Father in a garden. And it is fitting, too, that Mary Magdalene first encounters the Risen Lord in a garden.

"They're plowing the garden!"

It was the sound of soil being turned and seeds being planted. It was the sound of hope being renewed and life beginning again. Every time we witness new life and every time we

observe a new season, we see God in his garden. It reminds us that we too have been planted and are growing from death to life again.

Like that first Creation morning; like that first Easter, God walks in the garden with us and sows the seeds of surprise – the seeds of new life!

Reflection

1. What experience of "new life" have you had that brought you to a more intimate relationship with God?

2. Have you ever planted a garden or watched flowers gorw? What thoughts occurred to you?

3. What new seeds have been planted in your life recently? What was your experience of "the soil being turned" to make new growth possible?

What About Us?   *Matthew 19:23-25,27*

And Jesus said to his disciples, "Truly, I say to you, only with difficulty will a rich person enter the kingdom of heaven. Again I tell you, it is easier for a camel to go through the eye of a needle than for a rich person to enter the kingdom of God." When the disciples heard this, they were greatly astonished, saying, "Who then can be saved?" Then Peter said in reply, "See, we have left everything and followed you. What will there be for us?"

The apostles are "greatly astonished" when Jesus says how difficult it is for a rich person to enter the Kingdom of Heaven: "It is easier for a camel to pass through the eye of a needle." Clearly they don't interpret the "eye of the needle" to be the gate into the city of Jerusalem through which camels can pass, albeit with difficulty... nor do they seem to think Jesus is speaking symbolically. "Who then can be saved?" they want to know. And Peter asks bluntly, "What about us? We have given up everything and followed you." In answer, Jesus has some comforting words: "And everyone who has left houses or brothers or sisters or father or mother or children or lands, for my name's sake, will receive a hundredfold and will inherit eternal life." (Matt 19:29)

So... what about *us?*

How quickly we see ourselves among those who have "given up everything" and will "inherit eternal life"! How eager we are to count ourselves among those "last who will be first"! Like the old song says, we "want to be in that number / when the saints go marchin' in"! But perhaps we should bear in mind the ancient Jewish parable that maintains there is only a handful of righteous people in the world... and that presuming ourselves to be "in that number" is the very sin of pride that proves we are *not*.

So what about *us* ... who comprise 20% of the world's population, but consume 80% of its resources?

What about *us* ... who are so quick to "explain away" every passage of scripture that challenges us to change our lifestyle?

What about *us* ... who live in far greater luxury than the ancient landowners and kings to whom these passages were originally addressed?

What about *us* ... who peer from our gated communities in rich neighborhoods and never see Lazarus begging at our door?

What about *us* ... who believe that "sell all you have, and give it to the poor" was written for somebody else?

What about *us* ... whose riches may prevent us from entering the Kingdom?

I once read that, to capture monkeys in Africa, the natives attach small cages to trees. The cages are just big enough to hold a banana. The monkeys reach through the bars to grab the banana... but, when the monkeys try to depart with their prize, the banana won't fit through the bars. To escape, all they have to do is open their hands and let go of the banana! But the natives find the monkeys still there in the morning... held captive by their possessions.

What about us?

Henri Nouwen, a famous and popular Christian spiritual writer, speaks of living with "open hands." He reminds us that we are all born with our hands closed, our fists clenched, shouting "I!" "Me!" "Mine!" But, when we die,

our hands are open. Christian life, then, is about learning to let go. Christian life is learning to live with "open hands." Only when we have let go of everything – when our hands are truly open – only then, at last, can we "pass thorough the eye of a needle" and "inherit eternal life."

So… what about us?

What will *you* let go of this day?

To whom will you open your hands?

Reflection

1. The author uses the term "gated community" to refer to anything that separates us from those in need. What "gated community" do you live in? How do you protect yourself from contact with Lazarus who is "lying at your gate"?

2. How do you protect yourself from others getting too close? Why are you afraid to let others see you as you really are?

3. How do you feel about each of the "what about us" indictments in this reflection? Do you feel you are "one of the righteous"? Why or why not?

Walk Forth   Matthew 5:39

*But I say to you, do not resist the one who is evil. But
if anyone slaps you on the right cheek, turn to him
the other also.*

Willie Lohman, the central charter in Arthur Miller's classic
play "Death of a Salesman," always reminds me of a co-worker
I knew from my own early career in sales. Dale was a loud,
fast-talking, hard-drinking cash register salesman. On coffee
breaks, he often quoted scripture – but never without adding
his own interpretive tag line: "Turn the other cheek... and
you'll get smacked on the other side!" "Do unto others as
they would do unto you... but make sure you do it first!"
"The meek shall inherit the earth ... sure, a six-by-two plot!"
"The golden rule says... he who has the gold, makes the rules!"

Dale would never enter into a serious discussion about his
"interpretations" of scripture; he was obviously just working
the room for laughs. But I think that, deep down, Dale must
have felt that Jesus was a wimp and that his teachings were
not very practical in the real world. And one can certainly
get that impression from the popular renditions of some of
his sayings, or from some of the popular art that often depicts
Jesus as pale, fragile, or delicate-looking.

But we can be pretty sure that, as a carpenter living in hot
and arid Israel, Jesus was actually tanned, rugged, and strong.
The first century was a rough world, yet all kinds of people
were attracted to his preaching. It's hard to imagine that a
"wimp" would have attracted hard-working, salt-of-the-
earth fishermen, or the coarse, uncultured outcasts of society.
Scripture tells us that Jesus was considered "a glutton and a
drunk" (Luke 7:34) because he liked parties; he enjoyed
socializing with people. And if people didn't find his words
and teachings to be relevant to their daily lives, he certainly

wouldn't have attracted listeners by the thousands! So why would the masses be attracted to sayings like "turn the other cheek" or "the meek shall inherit the earth"? Those sayings don't sound very attractive to *me*, much less to a hard-working, first-century fisherman – or a hard-drinking, 20th-century cash register salesman!

Some scripture scholars, such as Andre Chouraqui, believe that our traditional translation of the beatitudes may be in error, inasmuch as those translations imply a kind of "passive consolation" in the face of trials. Chouraqui believes that the beatitudes are actually a call to action – an invitation to stand up, to arise and "walk forth," no matter what pain and trouble might lay ahead. Scholars who return to the Semitic terms underlying the Greek version of Jesus' words in this passage feel that the term "blessed" may be more properly rendered as "walk forth" – and certainly this translation gives a much more dynamic quality to the words of Jesus.

Walk forth, you meek and humble ones – for your gentleness is your strength. You shall inherit the earth because the earth has never been conquered by violence; your quiet legacy to others shall endure long after the works of the arrogant and self-important have passed away.

Walk forth, you who weep and mourn – for you shall be consoled. Your mourning is an indispensable condition for "walking forth" and getting on with your life; the pain you suffer shall one day be relieved, and by turning to others, you shall receive solace even as you teach sympathy.

Walk forth, those who thirst for justice – for you will be satisfied. The quest for fairness, equity, and righteousness is never-ending and you must never cease holding up the ideal; you must not hesitate to take action in your cause and you must never rest until justice is done for all.

Walk forth, you pure of heart – for you shall see God. You who always hold to your sense of purpose, who do not allow your souls to be dissuaded or distracted by deceptions, cynicism, or delusions; you shall indeed see God in the world all around you, and in face of every man and woman you meet.

Walk forth, you merciful ones – for you shall receive mercy. You who are sensitive and gentle, always willing to forgive others' wrongs; you who are not bound by rigid purism or fundamentalism... your compassionate example shall call forth mercy from the hearts of others and help to spread peace upon the earth.

Walk forth. Do not let yourselves be held back by fear, persecution, betrayal, or violence... walk forth and proclaim the kingdom! For it is in your "walking forth" – in your own growth and development, as much as in the blessings you bring to others – that you not only announce the kingdom that is to come... you help to bring it about!

Walk forth!

This interpretation of the beatitudes certainly does not portray a passive or submissive Jesus, but a Jesus that gives us a resounding call to action – a Jesus who is not telling us that we are "blessed" in our misery, but that we are blessed with qualities of love and mercy, and that we need to "walk forth" and carry those qualities into the world... so the work of the kingdom can begin!

Jesus is telling us that, in the end, the good guys win! And the "revolution" begins today! (Now *that's* a message I can imagine a crowd of thousands paying attention to!)

I wanted to tell all of this to my friend Dale... and I also wanted to tell him that a Christian doesn't turn the other cheek because he's weak and should be slapped on the other side!

"If someone strikes you on the right cheek, turn to him the other also" (Matt 5:39) – this passage isn't suggesting that we should give in to violence and let ourselves get beaten up; it's a call to stand firm against our enemies while holding fast to our purpose and identity as Christians. It's a call to be unwavering in the face of adversity and not lower ourselves to the level of the attacker. It's a call to be strong enough to return curses with blessings, injury with forgiveness, and hatred with love.

Hardly the path of a wimp!

"Turn the other cheek" is a non-violent response to a violent world – but more, it's an *anti*-violent response; it's a response that calls upon those doing the violence to *stop*. It is the path of justice and peacemaking; the path of Gandhi and Martin Luther King Jr. Dr. King knew all too well that the Christian life is not for weaklings. To live as a Christian is to live in protest! To love your enemies is to invite danger! To follow Jesus is to die for what you believe!

Walk forth!

Join the revolution!

Reflection

1. Does this reflection change your image of Jesus? In what ways?

2. As this reflection demonstrates, the beatitudes can be interpreted as a "call to action." Can you cite other examples from scripture where Jesus issues such a call?

3. Jesus seems to be saying that a Christian is to change the world by taking a stand, and taking action. What situation exists in your work life or personal life where you can remain true to the gospel by taking a stand, or taking action?

4. What call to action do you hear in your life today? What will you do in response to it?

Does the Ferry Still Run?

Jeremiah 14:17-18

You shall say to them this word: Let my eyes stream with tears day and night, without rest, over the great destruction which overwhelms the virgin daughter of my people, over her incurable wound. If I walk out into the field, look! those slain by the sword; If I enter the city, look! those consumed by hunger.

Matthew 13:43

Then the righteous will shine like the sun in the kingdom of their Father. Whoever has ears, let them hear.

It's 1964, and I'm 24 years old. I've been living out of a suitcase for almost two years, covering the deep South as a traveling auditor, and now I'm on my latest assignment in Louisiana.

"There's only two ways t'get ta Plaquemine, sonny," the toothless old man informs me as he fills my tank with gas. "You kin take da road north 90 miles and cross da bridge at Baton Rouge, or y'kin go down yonder 'bout a mile an' take the ferry 'cross da Mississippi. Either way, y'all bes' be gittin' back 'fore dark," was his parting counsel, alluding to the fact that I was a Yankee traveling alone during a troubled time in the South.

The hot August sun caused me to remove my suit jacket by the time the ferry reached mid-river. As I loosened my tie, I noticed a farmer with a horse standing near my car. On the other side was a guy with three sheep, a pig, and a few chickens. Mine was the only car on the ferry – and mine was *definitely* the only suit! "What am I doing here?" I wondered aloud.

Even more than when I had heard the old man's warning, I got the message – I was in the wrong place and in the wrong job. I wrote my resignation letter in the middle of the Mississippi River!

This passage from Jeremiah and the often-repeated words of Jesus, "Those who have ears, let them hear," both seem to call upon us to use our senses to observe what is going on around us, and to reflect on it... and take action! "Let my eyes stream with tears, day and night, without rest..." says Jeremiah. Our eyes would surely stream with tears if we opened them to the pain and suffering of our less-fortunate brothers and sisters, both around the world and in our own community. If we opened our eyes, we would surely see the destruction, the wounds, and the desolation that our self-centeredness, our self-indulgence, and our insensitivity have caused. Wherever we cast our eyes: "look! – those slain by the sword!" Everywhere we see: "look! – those consumed by hunger!" Throughout our world, we observe personal relationships sundered, lives squandered, natural resources plundered, children starved, whole populations bombed, "cleansed," wiped out. And all of this is happening while we live our oblivious lifestyles; all of this is happening while we peer from our gated communities. All of this is happening while we watch from the ferry, as we safely cross the river.

Throughout Matthew's gospel, the disciples often ask Jesus to explain his parables. But he usually concludes his explanation with a warning: "whoever has ears, let them hear." In modern political terms, Jesus has been consistently "on message" throughout his ministry – yet even his closest followers ask him to explain his words again and again. What should we hear? What did he say? Would you repeat that? Jesus has heard the questions before: "Am I my brother's keeper?" "Who is my neighbor?" "Is it lawful to

work on the Sabbath?" It seems that, when his followers don't like the answers they get, they simply ask the questions again!

What about us? Do we continue to ask the same questions because we don't like what we hear?

If we have ears that hear and eyes that see, we must live like Jesus. We must live with compassion and concern for our neighbors and the less fortunate. We must see the pain and hear the cries of anguish all around us, and not simply blot them out or ignore them. And we must recognize that *we* are part of the problem: in America, we constitute twenty percent of the world's population, but we consume eighty percent of the world's resources! We may not have caused all of the world's suffering, but we often foster it in many different ways, by the lifestyles we choose. We may not have created all of the world's problems... but how much have we really done to remedy them?

If we have ears that hear, we recognize the power of evil in the world but are not overwhelmed by it. We know we can't make it all go away, but we can reduce its hold on our lives and on the lives of those we encounter. We can remember that we are called to love, that we are called to lives of simplicity, compassion, and charity. Jesus challenges us to live "other-centered" lives, and to ease the pain of our sisters and brothers whenever and however we can.

"Whoever has ears, let them hear!"

Jesus seems to be saying, "It's not all that complicated!" If we listen to his words and open our eyes to the world around us, it will become quite clear to us what we must do. Perhaps that's why so many seem not to *want* to listen, or to see.

What about you? Will Jesus' words move you to a decision today? Will you listen and see? Will you take action?

Or does the ferry still run in Plaquemine?

Reflection

1. In what ways do you view life from "the ferry"? What barriers have you erected to separate yourself from people or situations that challenge your thinking or threaten your lifestyle?

2. How can you recognize when you refuse to listen or see?

3. How can you get in touch with the needs of the world, your city, your neighborhood? In what ways can you act to help meet those needs?

Stay in the Muck   Acts 14:19-20

Some Jews from Antioch and Iconium arrived and won over the crowds. They stoned Paul and dragged him out of the city, supposing that he was dead. His disciples quickly formed a circle about him and he got up and entered the city.

Much to my amazement, I'm suddenly the "old man" at the office! It seems like only yesterday that I was one of the thirty-something "young bucks," and the "old man" in the office was my friend John. John wouldn't describe himself as a strong Christian. He had gotten beaten up in church politics long ago and had withdrawn from institutional religion (and he wasn't even a Catholic!).

But John had a way of calling us "young bucks" back when we wandered from the path. When lunchtime gossip went too far, John would simply lay a small stone (which he always carried with him) on the table. Eventually someone would ask, "What's that?" John would quietly reply, "That's the 'first stone' – for the one of you without sin to cast!"

When John witnessed Christians doing un-Christian things to each other, he would give us "the score." I can still hear his sarcastic growl: "Lions, three – Christians, nothing!" John knew from his personal experience how vulnerable we are in the presence of other Christians. We expect our faith community to be a safe environment, a place where we can let down our guard. So when someone in that community hurts us, it's even more painful, because we expect better from them. We expect the Church to be different from "the world," and it's unsettling when we learn that, all too often, it's not. It's unsettling when we realize that the Church is, after all, nothing more than a gathering of sinners in search of forgiveness and hope.

In church work, burnout is very high – for staff as well as for volunteers. The people you serve sometimes stone you, and the rocks thrown from *within* the community always hurt more. It's understandable that so many people, like my friend John, withdraw from organized religion for this reason. But for me, the "me-and-thee-Jesus" approach is just too easy. Outside of a community, we live an un-confronted existence. There is no one to challenge our faith if we don't live in the "muck" of everyday Christian life. To live the Christian life fully, we must keep coming back to the table. We must stay "in the trenches" and apply the gospel to real world (and "real church") situations.

That's what Paul is doing in this reading from Acts. Then the "good Jews" from Antioch arrive and find that Paul is not preaching their brand of religion. Paul, however, feels empowered and doesn't ask their permission to pursue his ministry. And they get upset because he's doing something unorthodox – he's going against tradition; he's not obeying the rules. He's preaching to the Gentiles! As if God could love "them"! As if Jesus came to save "them"!

Paul is in trouble: he's being stoned by the very people he serves, and by the leaders of his community. He's being stoned by those who don't share his vision. The passage says, "His disciples quickly formed a circle about him..." His community of friends, those who *do* share his vision and believe in him, are there to protect him, support him, and give him strength. And the story continues, "He got up and entered the city." Paul went back into town, right back to the community that stoned him!

For most Christians, the surest way to God is through community. And not only through the community that loves us – sometimes our way to God is through the community

that misunderstands us, suspects our motives, or even the one that dislikes us, rejects us, threatens us, or hates us. Jesus pointed out that it is not the healthy who need a doctor, but the sick – and it may be that antagonistic, unfriendly community which most needs our witness, our support, and our love. I think it is this sense of mission that gives Paul the courage to "go back into town."

Being stoned isn't all bad. After all, it indicates that at least we are doing *something!*

We can't survive in this Christian life alone. Even Jesus needed support, which is why he chose his disciples. In the same way, we need the support of a community of friends. We need the support of a community that invites us to the table. We need the support of a community to give us the courage to get back in the "muck." We need the support of a community to give us the strength to, like Paul, "go back into town."

What community of friends will you seek out today?

Reflection

1. Think of a time when you were hurt, treated unfairly, or betrayed by someone in your Christian community. How did this affect you? How did you respond to the situation?

2. What doctrines or teachings of the church have been difficult or painful for you to accept? Why? How did (or do) you respond to them?

3. Given the hurtful experiences with religion that you may have experienced, why do you keep "coming back to the table"? How are you able to "go back into town"?

Honk if You Love Jesus   Matthew 7:21

*"Not everyone who says to me, 'Lord, Lord,' will enter
the kingdom of heaven, but the one who does the will
of my Father who is in heaven.*

I don't know how much fun it is to take long trips with kids
these days... it seems that they are too quickly relegated to
the back seat to watch DVDs or play video games. Gone are
the days of reading "Burma Shave" signs with them, or
counting down the miles to Wall Drug Store. Back when we
took our kids on family vacations, listing the states we saw on
license plates was a favorite pastime – second only to reading
bumper stickers!

Honk if you love Jesus!

The sticker's bold black letters were easy to read against its
bright yellow background, as the truck went around us on
our drive through the "Bible Belt" of northern Oklahoma.
"Is that a quote from the Bible, Dad?" came the question from
the back seat. "No, son," I replied. "The Bible says 'if you
love Jesus, love your neighbor' – anybody can honk!"

A paraphrase of Matthew 7:21 might say, "Not everyone
who 'honks' will enter the Kingdom of God." In other words,
we don't enter God's kingdom by making noise or by "talking
a good game," but by serving. Still, we Christians seem to
"honk" a lot! Maybe that's because it's so much easier to
"honk" than it is to help. After all, it's a lot easier to talk
about a person's problems than it is to help that person. It's
much easier to debate homosexuality than it is to be a friend
to someone who's gay. It's easier to discuss divorce than it is
to help those who are divorced. It's easier to argue about
abortion than it is to support an orphanage or an adoption
agency. And it's certainly easier to complain about poverty

and the welfare system than it is to help the poor. As Mark Twain sarcastically put it, "To be virtuous is noble... but to teach *others* to be virtuous is nobler – and no trouble!"

I have no doubt that when we Christians "honk" or shout "Lord, Lord," we usually do so with the best of intentions. But "good wishes don't pay the rent," as they say – so I often wonder what "the least of our brothers and sisters" would say about our good intentions.

I was hungry, and you formed a social action committee and discussed my needs.

Thank you.

I was imprisoned, and you went quietly to your chapel and prayed for my release.

I appreciate that.

I was naked, and you questioned the morality and appropriateness of my appearance.

It's nice that you are so concerned.

I was sick, and you knelt and thanked God for your own health.

In all things, give thanks.

I was homeless, and you preached about the shelter of God's love.

Look at the birds of the air: they neither reap nor sow.

I was lonely, and you left me alone and prayed for me.

What a friend we have in Jesus.

I know you are a good person. I know you strive to be close to God.

But I'm still hungry.

And I'm still cold.

And I'm still alone.

What are you going to *do* for me?

Reflection

1. When did you personally feed the hungry? Have you *ever* done so?

2. Do you engage the person that you are helping or just "flip them a dollar," in effect "honking" as you pass by?

3. What will you do to feed the hungry this month?

4. Other than physically, what are some other ways we can "feed the hungry"? How could you personally help to do this?

5. In what ways am I hungry? How do I make sure that my personal needs get met? How am I being "fed"?

Sell What You Have

Jesus said to him, "If you would be perfect, go, sell what you possess and give to the poor, and you will have treasure in heaven; and come, follow me."
Matthew 19:21

Again I tell you, it is easier for a camel to go through the eye of a needle than for a rich person to enter the kingdom of God."
Matthew 19:24

As Christians, most of us do our best to follow Jesus. But it's amazing how quickly our attitude can change when his words deal with the nature and use of wealth. How quickly and creatively we suddenly work to exclude ourselves from the story! "He's not talking about me," we tell ourselves; "I'm not rich!" (Never mind the fact that most people who live in America enjoy a far higher standard of living than any Biblical nobleman!) We look longingly to the patriarchs and kings of the Old Testament, we scour the Gospels for rich people who do not get condemned, and we console ourselves with the idea that even Jesus had wealthy friends.

Even those who otherwise insist on a literal interpretation of scripture hesitate when the text says to "sell everything you have and give it to the poor" (even though this passage is found in Matthew, Mark, and Luke – all of whom consistently present a negative image of wealth). Indeed, we sometimes get very creative in our efforts to make Jesus say something less challenging! We try to "shrink" the camel (by claiming that Jesus said "cable"), or we try to "enlarge" the needle (by declaring that Jesus was referring to a small gate in the wall of ancient Jerusalem called "the needle's eye"). We even try to "spiritualize" the passage or claim that Jesus was speaking symbolically, in a desperate effort to keep our pocketbook intact.

But I think the disciples must have taken Jesus' statement about the camel and the needle's eye literally. They react in "amazement" at such a rigorous requirement, and Jesus responds that this is indeed impossible without God. It's obvious that the disciples get the point because they then respond with a question about the adequacy of their own "leaving all." "See, we have left everything and followed you. What will we have?" (Matt 19:27).

The uncomfortable fact is that the message of Jesus is about making choices: "You cannot serve both God and Mammon (the ancient god of wealth)" (Matt 6:24, Lk 16:13). Jesus doesn't leave us much "wiggle room" when it comes to wealth and possessions, and we need to ask why. Why does he issue such a strong warning to the rich (as well to the rest of us, who – if truth be told – would *like* to be rich)?

Throughout the gospels, Jesus is very cautious about wealth and continually issues warnings against its temptations. Wealth can make us falsely independent – the community at Laodicea was warned about their attitude towards wealth and the false sense of security and control it gave: "For you say, I am rich, I have prospered, and I need nothing." (Rev 3:17) Timothy goes so far as to say that wealth can lead us "to ruin and destruction," and that we should "flee from it"! (1Tim. 6:9-11).

It's true that Jesus did have some rich friends, so it doesn't seem that he had a problem with wealth *per se*. The real issue seems to be what we *become* as we seek and amass wealth, the lengths to which we go (and the tactics we use) to obtain and protect it, how much we come to depend on it, and extent to which it separates us from those in need. An ancient Eastern proverb expresses this danger well: "Wealth enters the house as a slave... then it becomes a guest... then it becomes the master."

In the story of the rich man and Lazarus, the rich man is guilty of neglecting the poor man at his gate; it seems that his comfortable life, "clothed in purple and fine linen," contributed to his punishment (Luke 16:19-31). But despite the many warnings in scripture, we remain convinced that we can somehow "walk the line" and have it both ways – that we can serve both God and money. We tend to explain away Jesus' words, rather than seeking ways to live them out; we read into scripture the interpretation that justifies our chosen lifestyle, instead of lifting out the message that challenges us to change. In short, we interpret the clear but disturbing message of Jesus in light of everything else, rather than interpreting everything else in light of Jesus' message.

Jesus offers us an incomparable treasure, which no money can buy and no thief can steal. And he warns us that "where your treasure is, there will be your heart" (Matt. 6:21) – that our lust for material wealth will shackle us to this world unless we guard our heart and set our hope in eternal things.

Scripture offers us a paradox: those things we cling to we will lose someday, and the only things we will ever truly have... are what we give away.

What will you give away today?

Reflection

1. What do you think Jesus meant when he said, "sell all you have and give it to the poor"? Is that practical? Is it possible?

2. The reflection tells us of an Eastern proverb that says, "Wealth enters the house as a slave... then it becomes a guest... then it becomes the master." Consider each of these stages of wealth in your life. How do you know if material possessions, money, etc. have become the master of your life? What can you do to keep them from becoming your master?

3. What is the ultimate treasure "that money can't buy" and how does one acquire that treasure?

The Other Nine   *Luke 17:12-17*

And as he entered a village, he was met by ten lepers,
who stood at a distance and lifted up their voices,
saying, "Jesus, Master, have mercy on us." When he
saw them he said to them, "Go and show yourselves
to the priests." And as they went they were cleansed.
Then one of them, when he saw that he was healed,
turned back, praising God with a loud voice; and he
fell on his face at Jesus' feet, giving him thanks. Now
he was a Samaritan. Then Jesus answered, "Were
not ten cleansed? Where are the other nine?"

It seems they blew it, those other nine lepers that Jesus
cured – they didn't return to give thanks! But that doesn't
necessarily mean they weren't grateful. After all, who
wouldn't be glad to be free of the terrible effects of leprosy?
And I can't imagine that they weren't glad to be free of the
stigma of being outcasts, either. But in this passage, we don't
hear them say that – and neither did Jesus. Instead, only
one of the ten returned to give thanks. Now it's one thing to
be thankful or grateful; it's another to *express* our thanks.
Expressing gratitude draws us more deeply into a relationship
– especially when we say it to God, who has given us
everything we have. Those other nine, it seems, made no
effort to enter into a deeper relationship with Jesus.

Ok, so it was rude of them not to say "thank you" and they
missed an opportunity to know Jesus more fully. But let's
not write off the other nine too quickly! There may be some
things we can learn from them...

When Jesus directed the lepers to wash themselves in the
river, the other nine didn't ask any questions. They certainly
didn't ask the questions that we would likely ask: "Is this
some kind of joke? Why should we do that? How much water

should we use? Will it work if we just sprinkle?" No, the other nine simply listened to Jesus and "stepped out" in faith; they expected a miracle! But so often, we refuse to "step out"! We choose to stay in the security of the boat, frightened by the waves, and avoid leaving our "comfort zone." Refusing to "step out" is much worse than just forgetting to say "thank you"! If *we* could only be as faith-filled as those other nine were! They may not be able to teach us the fine points of etiquette or how to build closer relationships... but they do teach us to "step out" in faith! They do teach us to live in expectation – to trust in the promise and expect a miracle!

"Where are the other nine?" Scripture never answers this question, so we don't know. Maybe they're out there shouting the good news to everyone they meet! Maybe they're out there telling everyone what Jesus has done for them; how he changed their lives forever! Maybe they're out there spreading God's message of faith, hope, love, and healing!

Maybe they're out there saying "thank you" by the way they live their lives. Maybe they're out there teaching us how to live our faith.

And maybe – once the enormity of the gift they've been given sinks in – they'll realize that their relationship with Jesus is the true miracle.

Reflection

1. Who has had a defining impact on your life but does not know it? A teacher? A relative? A friend? Maybe it was the kind words of a minister or perhaps a stranger. In any case, what has kept you from acknowledging this gift, or saying thank you to this person?

2. In some cases, we may not be able to say thank you to the person who has affected our lives: we may not know their name, or cannot get in touch with them, or they may even have died. If there is such a person in your life whom you would like to thank in person but cannot, what are some ways in which you *can* say "thank you" to them?

3. While the "other nine" are not good examples of proper etiquette, they could provide us a good example of stepping out in faith. What might we learn about faith from the "ungrateful nine"?

Don't Get in the Way of Jesus   Acts 11:19-23

Now those who were scattered because of the persecution that arose over Stephen traveled as far as Phoenicia and Cyprus and Antioch, speaking the word to no one except Jews. But there were some of them, men of Cyprus and Cyrene, who on coming to Antioch spoke to the Hellenists also, preaching the Lord Jesus. And the hand of the Lord was with them, and a great number who believed turned to the Lord. The report of this came to the ears of the church in Jerusalem, and they sent Barnabas to Antioch. When he came and saw the grace of God, he was glad...

In 1972, Edward T. O'Meara was named the fourth Archbishop of Indianapolis. He often told the story of meeting Mother Theresa earlier in his career and asking what advice she had for a new bishop. Her answer to him was timeless, simple, and challenging.

"Don't get in the way of Jesus."

I'm always amazed how God's word is sometimes spread, and his work gets done, in the most unlikely ways. In this passage from the book of Acts, people are running for their lives to escape persecution after the stoning of Stephen – and God uses their fear to spread the gospel among the gentiles in Greece and beyond. It's amazing (and often humbling) to observe God's Spirit in action.

The story from Acts continues: the Antioch Gentiles are surprisingly responsive to the gospel message, and the number of those who believe grows enormously. "The news about them (the gentiles) reached the ears of the Church in Jerusalem, and they sent Barnabas to go to Antioch. When he arrived and saw the grace of God (at work), he rejoiced and encouraged them all."

Come Next Spring

Barnabas remembers the words of Jesus – "those who are not against us are for us" – and he recognizes the Antioch movement as the work of the Spirit. He advises the leaders to let the Spirit work, in effect telling them: *don't get in the way of Jesus!*

If only we as a church and as the people of God could better heed the example of St. Barnabas, and the words of Mother Theresa!

Gifted and holy people are often given limited voice in the church because of their marital status, gender, or other personal characteristics.

...don't get in the way of Jesus!

We watch as the number of priests and ministers dwindles, while we hold fast to our restrictive rules and traditions for ordination.

...don't get in the way of Jesus!

We become obsessed with definitions and denominational identity, and we only invite those to our table who profess our precise doctrines and adhere to our particular rituals.

...don't get in the way of Jesus!

We tear down our barns and build new ones while amassing possessions that speak to our fears, rather than using our less profitable gifts and talents that speak to our hearts.

...don't get in the way of Jesus!

We ignore poor Lazarus at our gate, enjoying our luxuries while others are denied necessities.

...don't get in the way of Jesus!

Scripture tells us that God's Spirit moves like the wind – "you hear the sound of it, but you do not know whence it comes or whither it goes" (John 3:8). The Spirit may not move in the ways of our traditions; the Spirit may move in ways that challenge us. Sometimes we may not even *like* the direction or manner in which the Spirit seems to be moving.

However, if good is being done, people are being brought to the Lord, and the work of the Kingdom is being carried out... then Mother Theresa and St. Barnabas would say to us:

...don't get in the way of Jesus!

Reflection

1. What doctrines, teachings, or attitudes of the church do you feel may be getting in the way of the gospel and the work of the Kingdom? How would you change those things?

2. When is a time that you feel you may have inadvertently "gotten in the way of Jesus"? How and why do you feel that happened? What can you do to ensure it doesn't happen again in the future?

3. What has happened in your life that has allowed others to see Jesus in you? What could you change in your life to more clearly reveal Jesus to another person or to the world?

Not One Stone   *Revelation 14:14-16*

*Then I looked, and behold, a white cloud, and seated
on the cloud one like a son of man, with a golden
crown on his head, and a sharp sickle in his hand.
And another angel came out of the temple, calling
with a loud voice to him who sat on the cloud, "Put in
your sickle, and reap, for the hour to reap has come,
for the harvest of the earth is fully ripe." So he who
sat on the cloud swung his sickle across the earth,
and the earth was reaped.*

The book of Revelation is, without a doubt, the most
misunderstood book in the Bible. Those who interpret
scripture in a literal way have a field day with its bizarre
images, dramatic language, and descriptions of catastrophic
events. It makes for popular movies and books about the
"end times" – and it frightens a lot of people. Given what
popular interpretation has done with the text, it's hard to
believe that this book was actually written as a message of
hope to a specific community of Christians, to help them cope
with the problems of their day. The "apocalyptic" literary
style in which the book is written is unfamiliar to us, and
interpretations that do not consider this style of writing or
the intent of the author take us down some strange roads –
and, in my judgment, lead to distortions and
misunderstandings of the text.

In my view, the book of Revelation has more to do with the
endings of "worlds" than it does with the end of *the* world.
Certainly, the book intends to shake us out of our doldrums
or complacency; it reminds us that worlds usually end with a
struggle, as we desperately cling to "the way things were." It
reminds us that our worlds *do* end – that nothing lasts forever.
Our personal world may end with the death of a loved one, or
a broken relationship. It may end with the loss of a job, with

172

a serious illness, or with the onset of a physical impairment. But in every case, our world is shattered and we scream, "I want my life back!"

As I watched the twin towers collapse on September 11, 2001, an apocalyptic passage that is found in each of the synoptic gospels kept running through my mind: *The day will come when not one stone will be left standing on the other.*" Our innocence and security collapsed that day. Or, more correctly, our *illusions* collapsed – the illusion that we were immune to harm, the illusion that we were in control of our lives, the illusion that we were safe from attack or unforeseen catastrophe. In a real sense, the world as we knew it came to an end that day.

The book of Revelation reminds us we cannot escape that end. Yet it also reminds us that when our world collapses – whether it be our personal world, our national world, or *the* world – we can still emerge with hope and renewed faith.

Despite its threatening imagery, the book of Revelation's final passages (Rev 22:17, 20) are a resounding message of hope: "The spirit and the bride say, 'Come.' Everyone who hears this must say 'Come.' Come, whoever is thirsty; accept the water of life as a free gift. He who gives testimony to all this says, 'Yes, indeed I am coming soon.' So be it. Come, Lord Jesus!"

We, too, can share in this message as we pray:

Come, Lord Jesus! Shatter my illusions, and give me hope.

Come, Lord Jesus! Destroy my security, and give me faith.

Come, Lord Jesus! Take away my stubborn independence, and give me trust.

Come, Lord Jesus! Shatter my world... that I might find my world in you.

Reflection

1. What does the phrase "Accept the water of life as a free gift" mean to you? Has there been a time in your life that you did not experience God's gifts as "free"? Why?

2. Describe a time in your life when your world collapsed. How did that occur? How was your hope restored?

3. How do you work toward the ideal, "that I might find my world in you"?

4. What "illusions" persist in your life? What would it feel like to let go of them? How would your life be different if you did?

God Falls   **John 13:21**

Amen, amen, I say to you, one of you will betray me.

"Judas betrayed Jesus and then committed suicide, so we know he's in Hell!" It was an unqualified and judgmental statement, but several people in the discussion group nodded their assent. I couldn't believe it – I felt that there was so much wrong with the statement, I hardly knew where to begin! "How can we possibly know that?" I wondered. "Who are we to presume to know the fate of *any* deceased person? Are we saying that someone who is so distraught as to commit suicide is fully responsible for his actions? What exactly do we mean by 'Hell,' anyway? And can we ever reach a point where we are beyond the mercy and saving power of God?" (No doubt my son, the philosophy major, would understand my skepticism and questions!)

It seems to me that Jesus could walk into *any* group of twelve people (or six, or three, or one) and say, "One of you will betray me" ...and someone would have to leave the room!

We don't know why Judas betrayed his Master. Was his treachery motivated by greed? By bitter disappointment? By disillusionment? Maybe Judas never intended for Jesus to die. Maybe he thought Jesus was proceeding too slowly, and not acting aggressively enough in setting up his messianic kingdom. Perhaps Judas only wanted to force the hand of Jesus by compelling him to act.

But in the final analysis, this story isn't about Judas anyway – it's about us. So, as I read the passage, I must ask myself, "How am I like Judas? Where am I in this story? How do I betray my Master?"

Perhaps the tragedy of Judas was his refusal to accept Jesus as he was. Ah ha! There I am! How often I, too, try to

manipulate God! How often do I try to control God, to change God's mind, to somehow compel God to do my bidding? Forget about "accepting his will" – I want God to answer my prayer and give me my miracle! Not only that, but I want him to do it *my* way, on *my* timetable! Judas would understand.

Deep down, I suspect there must be a better way to run the world, a better way to do things – after all, why should I have to suffer? God just doesn't do it right. He doesn't act the way I think God should act, and I'm not sure of his game plan. I'm not sure how things are going to turn out, so I try to take control. Judas would understand.

On the way to Calvary, Jesus falls to the ground! How can you trust a God who falls to the ground? Somebody should help him. I run from the room. Judas would understand.

God doesn't do it right. He doesn't do it the way *I* want. The Judas in me screams for him to change, to do it differently... to do it *my* way! But God will not change. He wants *me* to be changed by *him!* God is lying on the ground. God has his face in the dirt. He doesn't look much like God. How can I trust a God who lies on the ground? Judas would understand.

Hey, there's Simon! A human comes to the aid of God! God is in need! God calls for tenderness. God calls for mercy.

God calls for love.

God calls for me.

I am Simon, too – just a passer-by, who happens to be first on the scene. But I am the one God turns to. I am the one on whom God depends.

God falls... so that I may rise. Judas doesn't understand.

Do you?

Reflection

1. We are called to "judge not" – not Judas, not Hitler, not Osama bin Laden. Why?

2. What is your concept of Hell? If even notorious and known sinners are not beyond God's saving power, then who do you think is in Hell? Is anyone?

3. Judas could not reconcile his perception and expectations of Jesus with the actual *person* of Jesus. Can we? From the way we live our lives, which of Jesus' teachings is it clear that we reject?

4. In what ways do we try to control God? How can we work toward no longer making these attempts?

5. "Perhaps the tragedy of Judas was his refusal to accept Jesus as he was." How does this idea relate to question (1) above? And how do both ideas relate to trusting in God?

6. "God falls… so that I may rise." What does this statement mean?

Simple Words   Luke 6:46-49

*"Why do you call me 'Lord, Lord' and do not do what
I say? I will show you what he is like who comes to
me and hears my words and puts them into practice.
... But the one who hears my words and does not put
them into practice is like a man who built a house on
the ground without a foundation. ... it collapsed and
its destruction was complete."*

Simple words are often the most compelling. Any good writer
or editor will tell you that, most of the time, "less is more"
when it comes to language; extravagant exposition rarely grips
a reader's or listener's imagination as well as a clever turn of
phrase or a single perfect sentence. Hemingway knew this,
and so did Shakespeare. (And our author knew it too, by the
time I was finished editing his book!)

I think Jesus, skilled teacher and orator that he was, must
have known this as well. Whenever Jesus speaks in scripture,
he seems to measure his words carefully: his parables use
uncomplicated imagery, his assertions are clear and
straightforward, his admonitions are sharp, and his questions
are penetrating. He doesn't pull any punches; he lays it all
out for his audience and "tells it like it is" in no uncertain terms
– which is partly why he gets the Pharisees and Romans so
upset. And I think the above inquiry is one of his simplest
and most powerful: "Why do you call me 'Lord, Lord' and do
not do what I say?"

We often hear the parallel passage from Matthew's gospel,
that "Not everyone who says to me 'Lord, Lord' will enter
the kingdom of heaven," (Matt 7:21) but this version is far
more direct. The words Jesus uses in Luke's narrative
do not evoke a nebulous future or hereafter; they're
aimed straight at us, right here and now. And they ought

to resonate – they ought to echo down through the ages as a timeless rebuke, and be as much a verbal "slap in the face" to us in the present day as they were to the crowds of first-century Galilee.

They ought to sting. They ought to make us pay attention.

Jesus came into a world filled with poverty, suffering, oppression, greed, selfishness, turmoil, and brutality, and he brought a remedy: a simple message, expressed in the simple words recorded earlier in chapter six of Luke's gospel. Love your enemies. Do good, even to those who hate you. Turn the other cheek. Be merciful. Do not judge. Forgive. Do unto others as you would have them do unto you. And when Jesus spoke these simple words, people listened to them and praised him, and called him "rabbi," "teacher," "Lord," "Messiah," "Savior."

But Jesus asked them: "Why do you call me 'Lord, Lord' and do not do what I say?"

It isn't enough to listen. It isn't enough to understand, or to affirm, or to believe. It isn't enough to say "Lord, Lord." No, Jesus makes clear that we must hear his words, *and then act on them.*

And yet, more than twenty centuries after the words were first spoken, we still haven't learned. We still haven't acted. We still make war against our enemies. We still seek revenge when wrongs are done to us. We still deny the needs of the poor, hold grudges against others, and judge those who are different. We still live in a world filled with poverty, suffering, oppression, greed, selfishness, turmoil, and brutality. And we've been saying "Lord, Lord" for more than two thousand years!

We're still building our "houses" without a foundation. We still haven't done what he told us.

And so Jesus asks *us:* "Why do you call me 'Lord, Lord' and do not do what I say?"

Why indeed?

Will you do what he says today?

James R. Welter II

The Fourth Chapter:
Waiting for the Harvest

See how the farmer waits for the precious fruit
of the earth, being patient with it until it receives the
early and the late rains.
(Letter of James 5:7:10)

I'm sure that patience is a virtue – or at least it has been said so often that it has become common wisdom. But in my life, patience has always been in rather short supply. There is always an anxiousness in me to "get on with it," to "make things happen," to "take charge" and be in control.

"Waiting for the Lord" is a theme we find throughout scripture, and nowhere is it more evident than in the stories surrounding the birth of Jesus. We have the example of Anna waiting so many years for the coming of Jesus, keeping busy serving in the Temple while she waited, not knowing when the Christ – the Promised One – would come, nor what effect he would have on her life.

So it is with us. We live our ordinary lives: the traffic backs up at the stoplight, the phone rings, the TV or the CD blares in the background. We do our laundry, we buy our food, and we wash our dishes. Like Anna, we live in waiting, not knowing when Jesus will come to us. We don't know when he will arrive, nor what he will look like. He may come at midnight as a knock on our door; he may appear at sunrise with the challenge of a new day.

Come Next Spring

James R. Welter

He may look like a relative, a friend, a neighbor... he may be a stranger we meet on the road. He may even be reflected in the face of an enemy. And when he appears, we don't know the effect he will have on our lives, nor what he will ask of us.

But we have faith, and we live in hope.

And so we wait...

Love Made Visible   *1 Samuel 1:11*

*And she (Hanna) made a vow and said, "If you
remember me and do not forget me, if you give your
handmaid a male child, I will give him to the LORD
for as long as he lives."*

This passage from the book of Samuel is usually read at the
beginning of a new year. It speaks of those who longed and
waited for a child, and reconnects us with the stories of
Advent. The story of Elizabeth and Zechariah, who were
"advanced in age," comes to mind, as does the story of Simon
and Anna, who spent years in the temple waiting and praying
for the birth of Mary's child.

My wife and I walked that journey in a very special way as
we waited and longed for the birth of our first grandchild in
the winter of 2005. And what a special joy it was to finally
welcome Calvin Joseph Welter into the world at 11:49 p.m.
on Christmas Day! As we surrounded the hospital bed to get
our first glimpse of Calvin Joseph, emotions poured forth:
"Welcome to our world, Calvin!" "We've been waiting for you,
little guy! We love you." "Don't be afraid, we'll take care of
you." That night, the words of Advent seemed to be written
just for us: "A child is born to us, a son is given to us." "God
is with us." "Don't be afraid." "What will this child be?" "A
child shall lead them." Someone reminded us that there would
not be another day like that one, on which the feasts of
Christmas and Hanukkah converged, for another 400 years.
Suddenly even Isaiah's idyllic vision of peace – "the lion will
lie down with the lamb" – somehow seemed possible.

For some years now, I have been identifying with the "more
mature" characters as I read the stories in scripture. And
now, as a grandparent, I'm also experiencing that sense of

generational connectedness and the sense of life being "passed on" that is so often expressed in those stories.

The most enduring message I heard in the hospital room on that most special Christmas Day was the one spoken more than 300 times in both Hebrew and Christian scriptures: *"Do not be afraid."* It is spoken to the life that is beginning: "Do not be afraid – we have been waiting for you; we love you and we'll take care of you!" And it is spoken to the life that is ending: "Do not be afraid – we are waiting for you; we love you and we'll take care of you!"

Life is a circle. We have nothing to fear.

A Child is born to us – God's love made visible.

Reflection

1. Are there things in your life that cause you to be afraid? How do you deal with your fears? What hope or comfort do you get from scripture in this regard?

2. What message was passed on to you by previous generations in your life? How has it affected your life?

3. What message would you like to pass on to the next generation? Why?

The Hill Country   Luke 1:39

Mary traveled in haste to the hill country to a town of Judah, where she greeted Elizabeth.

"We'll meet at your house Saturday morning and drive up together." Our friend didn't have to mention where we were going; it was the first Saturday in December and we already knew. Our gourmet group, which had formed during the holidays more than twenty-five years ago, was making its 17th annual trip to Ft. Wayne to spend the day with our friends who had moved there years before. It was once a caravan – we would crowd into several cars and follow each other north up Highway 69, stopping at the coffee shop in Anderson and laughing to see who would show their AARP card for a senior discount.

"Mary traveled to the hill country..." The hill country is always a difficult journey and few would choose to travel that road. But visiting her cousin Elizabeth was important so, "Mary traveled in haste to the hill country."

This time, our trip was different: some people had moved away, and for the second consecutive year, someone in our group had died. In all, four were now gone. This year, we traveled in one car, and no one mentioned the coffee shop in Anderson – the joke wasn't funny any more. There seemed to be an unspoken haste to reach our friend's house.

That evening, wine was poured and we raised our glasses. "May our numbers be no fewer next year"; it was more a prayer than a toast. We were in our "hill country" – a difficult place through which we would prefer not to travel – and the words of Ezekiel (6:8), "I will leave a remnant in your midst," were never more real.

Grief is more painful during the holidays. Many "travel to the hill country" in the holiday season – the road is crowded, yet few are "greeted" in their grief. It has been ten holiday seasons since my mother and my sister Fran died, and there is something about those anniversaries that makes it all seem real again. The pain is every bit as great: it feels as though that unopened Christmas present still lays in the back seat of our car, just as it did ten winters ago.

But I know from workshops on grief that I have attended – and from scripture – that it's OK to "cry out" this Advent season; it's OK to shout at these hills. For many, this will be their first holiday season without a loved one. For others, it will be their third, or fifth, or tenth – the pain doesn't go away. For still others, there is no "greeting" – they are completely alone in this holiday season. Amidst all of this suffering, Isaiah urges us to "cry out"! (Is 40:6) He invites us to acknowledge our pain while offering us hope in the One who is to come. Isaiah tells us it's OK to cry this Advent, this Christmas; it's OK to "cry out" in your "desert." To cry when that special song is sung, to cry for the empty place at the table, to cry as you hang that special angel on the tree. To cry for Christmas as it was last year, or the year before – to cry for Christmas as it will never be again.

Our hearts hold the pain, struggles, yearnings, and desires that lie deep within. Isaiah urges us to cry out to God in the sadness, grief, joy, hope, and yearning of our hearts. Isaiah has spoken to us in these Advent weeks, telling of God's dwelling with us. He proclaims, "Comfort, give comfort to my people" (Is 40:1). He tells us that, if we hope in the Lord, we "will run and not grow weary, walk and not grow faint." (Is 40:31). He assures us that the Lord is with us, and that "like a shepherd he feeds his flock and gathers the lambs in his arms" (Is 40:11).

Mary "traveled in haste to the hill country" to live out the message that Isaiah has proclaimed: "A young woman will bear a son and he shall be called Emmanuel – which means 'God is with us.'"

Come, Lord Jesus!

Reflection

1. What are some of your family's holiday rituals? How did they originate and who is involved in them? When did you realize their importance in your life?

2. How have your rituals changed over the years? How do you feel about those changes?

3. Reflect upon some of the "travels to the hill country" in your life. How have these experiences changed you? How have they affected your faith?

You Are My Beloved   Luke 3:21-22

Now when all the people were baptized, and when Jesus also had been baptized and was praying, the heavens were opened, and the Holy Spirit descended on him in bodily form, like a dove; and a voice came from heaven, "You are my beloved Son; with you I am well pleased."

If you asked me to list the two most important things I have learned from scripture, it would be these: God loves us, and Jesus was truly human. God's love is made manifest to us in Jesus, who is called "Emmanuel" – "God with us." The significant phrase here is "with us" – God is not just visiting, passing through, or looking over our shoulder. He is *with us* in the person of Jesus, who was truly human.

In other words, Jesus was not God merely "pretending" to be human; he was not God "in disguise" or somehow feigning mortal status. In short, Jesus was, as the Apostles' Creed puts it, "true God and true man" – which means that he was as fully human as you or I. (The fact that the scriptures say Jesus performed miracles is no argument against his humanity; they say that the apostles, the prophets, and other human beings did also.) As one of us, Jesus knew hunger and thirst, joy and sorrow, pleasure and pain, just as we do. And when he was tempted – he *could* have sinned! When he was called to his ministry, he *could* have said no! When he faced a moral choice, he *could* have chosen to do wrong! (If he could not have made those choices, then he would have lacked free will and could not have been a true human being.)

And his emotions were human, too: he grieved at the death of his friend Lazarus, he enjoyed the friendship of his disciples, and he sweat blood in the garden of Gethsemane because he was afraid and wasn't sure what was going

to happen! He is Emmanuel: he is with us and one of us. Jesus understands our lives and our struggles, not because he was God and knew all things, but because he was human and *experienced* all things.

If we understand that Jesus was fully human and faced the same situations in life that we do – if we realize that he had no "special advantage" and (as scripture shows) couldn't simply play his "God card" every time he got into trouble – then we can learn something from his life. Rather than thinking of him as "above" us, we can think of him as *among* us. Rather than thinking he could not fail and being dismissive when we hear of his temptation, we can instead ask how he *resisted* that temptation and can seek the source of his strength.

In Luke's gospel, the baptism of Jesus (Lk 3:21f) takes place just before his temptation in the desert (Lk 4:1f), and the two events cannot be separated. The affirmation Jesus hears at his baptism – "You are my beloved son" – provides him with a sense of identity and gives him the strength to resist the temptations that are to come.

There was nothing new or unique about the kinds of temptations that Jesus faced in the desert. Every temptation is the same: it is an invitation to "come into my world" and accept what is offered. Come into my world and accept my values; come into my world and accept my lifestyle; come into my world and accept my agenda and priorities. So the temptations of Jesus are the same temptations that we face: the temptation to accept the values of the world, to identify with them and the agenda they set, and to use our abilities in their service.

"Turn this stone into bread" – *do* something to meet your own needs, then you will have value. "Worship me and the

world's kingdoms will be yours" – make material wealth and earthly power your highest values, and you'll end up rich and important. "Jump from the Temple" – do something flashy to impress people so they'll speak well of you, and you'll become famous and admired. Do these things and you will have value; do these things and you will be loved.

But Jesus remembered his Father's words: "You are my beloved." And Jesus believed those words. So when the world said "do something and you'll have value," Jesus said, "I don't have to do anything; I know who I am. I am the beloved – and I already have value." And when the world said, "make wealth your goal and you'll be rich," Jesus said, "I don't need material wealth; I am the beloved – and I am 'rich' already." And when the world said, "do something flashy to impress us, and you'll be famous," Jesus said, "I don't need your praise and approval; I don't get my identity from you. I already have the only praise and approval that matters – I am the beloved of God!"

If we believe that the words spoken to Jesus are also spoken to us, then the world's temptations can't touch us! So when you lose your job and the world says, "you're not productive any longer, so you're nothing and have no value," you can say with Jesus: "Yes I do, because I know who I am – I am the beloved!"

And when your spouse dies, your friends leave, or your children grow up and move away, and you feel empty and alone, you can still say that life is worth living, because "I am the beloved!"

And when you finally grow old, your health fails, and the world says you are of no importance to anyone, you can say with Jesus: "Yes I am … I am the beloved of God!"

Stand before your mirror today and hear the words spoken to Jesus... hear the words spoken to you!

"You are my beloved... with you I am well pleased."

Reflection

1. What examples in scripture helps you to know and understand Jesus as fully human?

2. Do you believe that Jesus really could have sinned? Why or why not?

3. How does your belief about Jesus' ability or inability to sin make a difference in your relationship with him?

4. "I am the beloved son / daughter of God." What feelings does this statement invoke in you?

The Cry of the Poor   Psalm 34 (Song Refrain)

The LORD hears the cry of the poor. Blessed be the Lord!

"We don't have enough food to go around tonight." My mother, a single parent, was letting us kids know the situation we faced... again. "Why don't you boys go help Doc (our neighbor) with his cows, and maybe he'll invite you to stay for supper." It was an easy walk to Doc's place, just a mile down the gravel road that passed through our farm.

"What if he doesn't ask us to stay and eat?" I asked my older brother as we approached the familiar farmhouse. "We won't leave until he does," came the reply. "And be sure to say you're really hungry, so he'll fix a lot of food. That way, we'll have some left over to take home for Mom and the girls."

It was a walk that no eight-year-old should ever have to make. And it involved survival skills that no kid should ever have to learn.

"The LORD hears the cry of the poor!" When I sing or read that refrain, my first reaction is: "Then why doesn't he do something about it?" As an adult and a believing Christian, I realize that it isn't a matter of the Lord hearing our cry — rather, it's a problem of the Lord finding an open heart that is willing to respond.

A common question for Christian sharing groups during Advent is, "what are you waiting for?" And we sit in our warm, comfortable homes, maybe with a fire in the hearth, surrounded by friends, and share our anticipation of the holidays. We'll take time to visit friends, the kids will be home, our family has certain traditions, and we'll celebrate and go to church together. Those are the things we wait for during Advent, and those are all good things.

But that's not what the question is about!

Advent is a time of waiting. And the question for every Christian is, "what are you *waiting* for?" There's no need to wait for a holiday or a special occasion – you can be the presence of Christ in the world right now! You can make Jesus real to someone *today*. What are you *waiting* for? You can assist a pregnant woman, you can welcome a stranger; you can answer the knock on your door. What are you *waiting* for? You can feed the hungry, visit the sick, give to someone in need, or make a difference in someone's life!

Right now!

We know that "the LORD hears the cry of the poor." The question is: do *we* hear the cry of the poor?

It's Advent... what are we *waiting* for? Christ can be born in us today. In this hour. In this moment.

If we open our hearts... if we hear the message of Christmas... if we hear the cry of the poor... if we allow Jesus to be born in us today, right now... we can make a difference.

And maybe somewhere, this year... an eight-year-old child won't have to walk down a gravel road.

Reflection

1. In what ways do you "hear the cry of the poor"? What could you do to respond to it?

2. In what ways would you like your faith community to respond to the poor? How could you help?

3. What are you "waiting for" this Advent season?

4. What, for you, is the over-riding message of Advent this year?

Ask and You Shall Receive   Matthew 7:7-8

"Ask, and it will be given to you; seek, and you will find; knock, and it will be opened to you. For everyone who asks receives, and the one who seeks finds, and to the one who knocks it will be opened."

We've all laughed at the joke – we've heard it in homilies or had it forwarded to us by e-mail. A man is caught in a flood and, as the waters rise, his neighbors encourage him to get in their car and leave with them. He dismisses their warning and tells them he isn't worried. "God will save me," he declares. The waters continue to rise and a rescue team in a boat approaches. "Get in," they yell, but the man waves them off, shouting, "God will save me!" Finally, as the waters get higher, he is on the roof of his house and a helicopter is hovering overhead. A rope ladder is dropped and the rescuers entreat the man to grab the rope and climb up. He refuses and bravely shouts, "Don't worry, God will rescue me!" The waters rise further and the man drowns. When he meets God in Heaven, the man asks, "Why didn't you save me?" And God responds, "I sent you a car, a boat, and a helicopter – what more do you want?!"

As with most humor, this story is funny because it reflects our own nature. It reflects the fact that we don't always recognize God working though other people. And it reflects the fact that we usually pray with our own agenda in mind. Like the man in the joke, we limit ourselves to the answer that *we* want. And we insist that things come to us in a certain way. We know the response we want, and we will accept no other!

We pray for more priests but restrict their gender and lifestyle. We will accept no other. We pray for generous hearts but decide that generosity will be used to meet our financial

goals, build our buildings, or support our favorite ministry. We will accept no other. We light candles so people will be healed, and we stay in the chapel on our knees so they will be safe. It should work, we think – after all, the Bible says "Ask and you shall receive! Knock and it will be opened!" We will accept no other.

My life experience tells me that sometimes prayer seems to work that way – but that, most often, it doesn't. We pray for someone to live, but they die anyway. We pray for a promotion, but we don't get it. We pray that it won't rain on our special day, but it does!

"Ask and you shall receive!" There are those who interpret this passage as some sort of guarantee from God, believing that if you don't get what you ask for, it's because you didn't pray hard enough or you didn't have enough faith. Try telling that to a young mother whose spouse has just died of cancer, or to the person who just lost their job. Or explain to someone who is dying of thirst why I get rain so my grass will grow! Does the rain on my lawn mean that God likes me best? And what about those opposing teams – or sides – who are praying for opposite things? Does God play favorites? Does the one with the most faith win?

I'm sure the disciples also experienced these ambiguities of life, and wondered why their prayers didn't seem to work very well. They see Jesus praying one day and they ask, "Lord, teach us to pray." (Luke 11:1). Seeing how Jesus prays (especially in Luke's gospel) challenges me to remember what "taking something to God in prayer" really means.

True prayer – which is always answered – is not praying for what *I* want. True prayer is not praying for the cup to pass; God didn't promise that and didn't grant it even to his Son.

True prayer involves remembering that I don't pray to change God's mind; I pray to change my heart. It means praying like Socrates, asking only that God give me what is best for me – and trusting that God knows what is best far better than I do. It means praying like the Eastern mystics, who asked only to be granted the trials and suffering they needed to purify their souls and awaken their compassion for others. It means praying so I can let go and release my burden, and praying for the strength to accept whatever comes and the wisdom to grow from that experience.

It means praying for what God *does* promise to give: strength, courage, hope, and freedom from anxiety and fear.

I pray for the faith to take God at his word.

Reflection

1. What does it mean to you to pray? How have you come to your understanding of prayer?

2. If the way you pray has changed, *how* has it changed? And how has it changed your life?

3. Consider a time when your heart was changed by prayer. How did this come about?

Nothing You Can Do   *Luke 15:11-12*

*And he said, "There was a man who had two sons.
And the younger of them said to his father, 'Father,
give me the share of property that is coming to me.'
And he divided his property between them."*

It's 1998, and the RCA Dome in Indianapolis is filled to capacity. Sixty thousand people in one place is always an impressive sight – but when they gather to hear the preaching of the gospel, it's not only impressive, but inspiring. The crowd senses that this is the last time Billy Graham will be in our town; he is now an old man and is obviously in the winter of his ministry. The "warm-up" minister startles the crowd with an invitation: "Turn to the person next to you and say, 'God loves you – and there's nothing you can do about it!'" Nervous hesitation gives way to wide grins and the invitation becomes a roar as sixty thousand people share the good news: "God loves you – *and there's nothing you can do about it!"*

One of the unique characteristics of Luke's gospel is his use of contrasts and comparisons. If we are reading gospel passages of things lost and found or the first being last, we can be sure that Luke is the author. It is Luke who gives us the story of the tax collector and the sinner, the woes contrasting with the blessings of the Beatitudes, and the story of the rich man and poor Lazarus.

Luke is the only gospel writer to tell the story of the Prodigal Son, which contrasts the younger and older brothers and their understanding of love. In this parable, Luke provides a unique insight into the nature of God's love for us.

Most of us are familiar with the story: the younger son asks for his inheritance and journeys to a "far country," where he "squandered his property in reckless living." Finally he is at

rock bottom and "was longing to be fed with the pods that the pigs ate." But when he came to his senses, he said, 'How many of my father's hired servants have more than enough bread, but I perish here with hunger!'" And so he devises a plan: "I will arise and go to my father, and I will say to him, 'Father, I have sinned against heaven and against you. I am no longer worthy to be called your son. Treat me as one of your hired servants.'"

We usually think of this parable as a story of forgiveness – and it is – but another lesson is intertwined here, and it comes at the very end of the story. Luke doesn't really conclude the story; rather, he keeps us hanging like one of those movies with a surprise ending. In the closing scene, the father is in a dilemma. On the one hand, his youngest son is saying, "You can't love me! I've squandered your money, I've ruined your reputation; I've lived with a married woman, and even now I'm a drunk! You *can't* love me after what I have done!" And on the other hand, his oldest son is saying, "Hey, what gives? You're throwing a party for that son of yours? (He doesn't even call the younger man his brother – he calls him "that son of yours"!) You're throwing a party for him, after what he has done?! What about *me?* I've stayed with you all these years and worked the farm! I've taken care of my wife and family; we go to the synagogue every week. You've *got* to love me – I've earned it!"

And the father is shaking his head. They don't understand, he thinks. Neither of my sons understands what I mean when I say I love them.

The father is right – his sons don't understand. They don't know what sixty thousand people confessed that night in the RCA dome: God loves you – and there's nothing you can do about it! No matter what sin you commit, God won't love

you any less. You can rob a bank, kill people, abandon your family – and God won't love you any less. He loves Charles Manson, Saddam Hussein... he loves Osama bin Laden as much as he loves you! The younger brother didn't understand that.

God loves you... and there's nothing you can do about it.

And it doesn't matter how good you are, either – God won't love you any more. You can sell all you have and give it to the poor; you can devote your entire life to the homeless in the streets of Calcutta – and God won't love you any more than he does right now. He loves you as much as he loves the Pope, or Mother Theresa... or even his own Son! The older brother didn't understand that.

This is the good news that Jesus brought when he came ... and this is the good news that Jesus brings to us today. He says, "God loves you... but not in the way that *you* love! God loves you without any conditions, without any limitations; he loves you no matter what you do, or don't do... he loves you more than you can imagine, and he always has. God loves you like a Father loves his Son... he loves you now... and his love... will never end."

God loves you.

And there's nothing you can do about it!

Reflection

1. With which character in the story of the prodigal son do you most identify? Why?

2. "God loves Osama bin Laden as much as he loves you!" What emotions does this statement invoke in you? Why?

3. If God doesn't love us any more than he currently does, no matter how good we are, then why should we try to "do good"?

Just Say Thank You   Luke 21:1-4

*Jesus looked up and saw the rich putting their gifts
into the offering box, and he saw a poor widow put
in two small copper coins. And he said, "Truly, I tell
you, this poor widow has put in more than all of them.
For they all contributed out of their abundance, but
she out of her poverty put in all she had to live on."*

It is sometimes difficult for us to accept gifts. We have been
taught to "just say thank you," but our other comments often
betray our discomfort: "Oh, you shouldn't have!" "I can't
accept this!" "I didn't bring anything for you!" Little wonder,
then, that we also have trouble grasping the concept of
salvation as a gift! We "can-do" Americans seem more
comfortable with the idea of "earning" salvation – just as our
traditional work ethic leads us to earn good grades, an income,
a raise, a promotion, or other rewards. We may sometimes
wish that God would spell out an exact list of tasks or "do's
and don'ts" for salvation, so we could know exactly where we
stand and exactly what we must do to earn our heavenly
reward! And some well-intentioned religious people can make
it seem just that easy: say a simple prayer, they may tell us;
pray a devotion, receive a sacrament, and you've "got it"!
Yet scripture teaches us that salvation isn't something we
can earn no matter what we "do" – and we are uncomfortable
with the idea that salvation is not under our control. It seems
we've never quite forgotten our childhood experience of good
deeds being tracked and rewarded, or gotten past the cultural
idea that we can "work our way" toward whatever prize we
desire.

In this passage, Jesus commends the widow who "gave
everything she had" as an offering. However, he never
suggests that this is the key to salvation, nor does he imply
that she earned anything for herself by making that gift. In

the pre-Vatican world of the 1950s, we Catholics did a lot of counting: we counted our sins (and sorted them by severity), we counted our prayers (three "Our Fathers" and three "Hail Marys"), and we counted indulgences (40 days). (If you don't know what any of that means, just say "Thank you, Lord!")

As a Catholic who was raised in that era, I grew up convinced that God was a scorekeeper (if not a CPA!). I was 35 years old when I first heard a priest say "God loves us and doesn't keep track of our sins... and not only that," the priest went on, "but you don't have to earn salvation – he gives it to you for free." I couldn't believe it! I had never heard this message before (at least, not from a Catholic). I went home and ripped through my Bible with a vengeance, looking for every passage that spoke of salvation as a gift. And – praise Jesus! – I found many, many such passages.

One passage from Revelation alludes to this saving gift: "No one could learn this hymn except the hundred and forty-four thousand (a symbolic number meaning the people of God) who had been ransomed from the earth. These are the ones who follow the Lamb wherever he goes. They have been ransomed as the first fruits of the human race for God and the Lamb." In other words, God offers us salvation through Jesus. We do not earn it; we *cannot* earn it – it is God's free gift. We only have to accept it!

Can we love and trust God enough to allow him to give us salvation? Our life of good works and service to others is certainly praiseworthy, but it is its own reward – it does not earn us "points" toward "victory" in some celestial game! The Christian life we lead is our response to, and signifies our acceptance of, God's free gift of salvation – it is our perpetual "thank you" to the Lord; it is the Eucharist we live and become.

One writer put it this way: "We are not true Christians until we can give up the illusion of heaven." In other words, we are not true Christians until we stop counting and measuring and doing good deeds to try to "work" or "earn" ourselves a heavenly reward; we are not true Christians until we can trust completely in God's love and mercy, and can love and serve others in response to what we have *already* been given. We cannot be true Christians until we love "because God first loved us."

Salvation is God's free gift to us... it is up to us to learn how to just say "thank you"!

Reflection

1. Respond to the phrase "We are not true Christians until we can give up the illusion of heaven." What is this "illusion" and how can we work toward giving it up?

2. In another scripture passage, the laborers who "worked all day in the vineyard" were angry because those who came late were given the same reward (Matt. 20:1-16). How do you feel about those who live a carefree (or even sinful) life, yet may also receive the "free gift" of salvation? How does this reflect your attitude toward "earning" salvation?

3. What concept of salvation were you taught as a child or young person? Was that concept comforting? Did it scare you? What image of God did it create in your mind?

4. How is your understanding of salvation different from that of other Christian traditions? How is your current understanding of salvation different from that which you may have held earlier in life?

Our Father   ***Matthew 6:7-10***

"And when you pray, do not heap up empty phrases as the Gentiles do, for they think that they will be heard for their many words. Do not be like them, for your Father knows what you need before you ask him. Pray then like this:

"Our Father in heaven, hallowed be your name. Your kingdom come, your will be done, on earth as it is in heaven."

Many times, our prayers betray an effort to control God. This may not be an effort that we make deliberately, nor even an attitude that we're fully conscious of having – but what we say in prayer often makes the truth very clear. In praying, we often try to "bargain" with God: "If you grant me this, I'll do that," "If you spare me pain, I'll be more faithful." But prayers like these are just thinly disguised attempts to "persuade" God to give us what *we* want! Even so, Jesus understands: in the garden, he sweats blood as *he* wrestles with the "whys" and asks for a miracle! "Let this cup pass," he prays. But, finally, he ends his prayer with "your will be done."

Jesus tells his disciples, "Your Father knows what you need before you ask him." But then, one might well ask: why pray at all? Indeed, the words we say in prayer are not for God's benefit – he already knows our feelings and needs better than we do. But he still wants us to speak to him from the depths of our hearts in prayer, so that we can see into *ourselves*; so we can recognize and accept the nature and depth of our own feelings. And when we do this, prayer changes *us* – so that we can accept God's will for us, as Jesus did, and be open to his healing grace... and can work with him to bring about his

kingdom here on earth. Our lesson from the garden, then, is that we do not pray to change God's mind – we pray to change our hearts.

If I truly pray to change my heart...

I cannot say *OUR* if my religion has no room or acceptance for strangers, their ways, and their needs.

I cannot say *FATHER* if I do not demonstrate this relationship to God through my daily living.

I cannot say *WHO ART IN HEAVEN* if all my interests and pursuits are of earthly things.

I cannot say *HALLOWED BE THY NAME* if I do not give God respect, honor, glory, and trust.

I cannot say *THY KINGDOM COME* if I am unwilling to help his kingdom grow in my heart, in my home, in my church, in my community, in my country, and in my world.

I cannot say *THY WILL BE DONE* if I am resentful of having God's will imposed on my life.

I cannot say *ON EARTH AS IT IS IN HEAVEN* unless I am ready to give myself over to God's service right here and right now – always.

I cannot say *GIVE US THIS DAY OUR DAILY BREAD* unless I expend my own honest efforts for it, or if I ignore the everyday needs of my brothers and sisters.

I cannot say *FORGIVE US OUR TRESPASSES AS WE FORGIVE THOSE WHO TRESPASS AGAINST US* if I continue to hold a grudge or persist in a quarrel with anyone.

I cannot say *LEAD US NOT INTO TEMPTATION* if I do not make honest efforts to *avoid* temptation, or if I choose to remain in a situation where I am likely to be tempted.

I cannot say *DELIVER US FROM EVIL* if I support, or allow myself to be part of, systems that are oppressive or result in injustice.

I cannot say *AMEN* unless I can say, "Whatever the price, this is my prayer – thy will be done!"

Can you say this prayer today?

Reflection

1. The "Lord's Prayer" consists of seven petitions. List those petitions and, beside each, write how you would like to see that petition answered in your life.

2. Now go back, and beside each petition, write how you intend to *become* part of that answer in your own life or in another person's life!

The Cup   Luke 11:37-41

After he had spoken, a Pharisee invited him to dine at his home. He entered and reclined at table to eat. The Pharisee was amazed to see that he did not observe the prescribed washing before the meal. The Lord said to him, "Oh you Pharisees! Although you cleanse the outside of the cup and the dish, inside you are filled with plunder and evil. You fools! Did not the maker of the outside also make the inside? But as to what is within, give alms, and behold, everything will be clean for you."

"Whenever we hear the word 'Pharisee,'" the preacher began, "we should substitute the word 'Christian'!" It was an attention-grabbing opening line that would be the envy of any public speaker. But he also made a good point: historically, the Pharisees were decent, well-intentioned, solid citizens – a bit smug, perhaps, but not villains. Yet, any people who declare themselves better than others, or more possessed of truth and virtue, run the risk of gliding from decency to smugness, from satisfaction to self-serving, from conviction to cruelty.

Like the Pharisees, we too sometimes undermine the ministry of Jesus. Our quest for certainty goes beyond physical security – we often want protection against change, new ideas, uncomfortable truth, doubts, and honesty. It is we, the prosperous and satisfied, who turn away when Jesus strays from our path. It is the orderly and solid citizens who often feel threatened by the radical and disruptive message that Jesus preaches.

And it *is* a radical message. Jesus makes extravagant claims on people's lives: new names, new occupations, new homes, new priorities, and new attitudes toward wealth and power.

It's not the easy road of judging other people's morality, but a call for a wrenching examination of our own lives, behaviors, motives, and vices. Clean the *inside* of the cup, he tells us today.

"Cleaning the inside of the cup" must go beyond a mere listing of our sins, or acknowledgements of our shortcomings. We must be willing to come to grips with the root cause of our sins: our addictions, our fears, and our failures. Cleaning the inside of the cup is about letting go. It's about letting go of the fears that enslave me, and the addictions that bind me. It's about letting go of the possessions that secure me, and the hatreds that fill me. Inside the cup, I must let go of the familiar, the comfortable, and the settled.

It is the road less traveled. It is a fearful, uncertain, and painful journey. It is why we prefer the rituals of religion to the wilderness of faith. It is why we fight to retain the familiar: our traditions, orthodoxy, rituals, and rules. Inside the cup, we must go to Moriah – to the desert, to the mountain. Here, we are asked not only to give up our sins and offenses, but to give up our certainties and our inheritance as well.

Inside this cup, we must push to the very center of our self until we hear the Lord asking, "What do you want from me?" Inside this cup, we must answer as honestly as a blind beggar wanting sight, and as boldly as a widow demanding justice. Here, we will not be beaten up with haughty words and harsh definitions, nor shackled by the expectations of others. Here, we will be listened to, and loved, and taught.

Inside the cup, we learn to live without simple answers. Inside the cup, we dare to venture beyond certainty and safety. Inside the cup, we see more than we could imagine. Inside the cup, we hear the Lord calling our name.

Are you willing to look inside your "cup" today?

Reflection

1. What "certainty" have you have you had to give up in looking inside your "cup"?

2. Rituals and traditions make us feel comfortable and secure. Has there been a time when you have challenged a ritual or tradition in your faith journey?   What was the outcome of that challenge?

3. What have you discovered in the center of your "cup" that has challenged you in your faith journey?

My Father's Robe   Luke 15:20-22

And he arose and came to his father. But while he was still a long way off, his father saw him and felt compassion, and ran and embraced him and kissed him. And the son said to him, "Father, I have sinned against heaven and before you. I am no longer worthy to be called your son." But the father said to his servants, "Bring quickly the best robe, and put it on him, and put a ring on his hand, and shoes on his feet."

There is an old bathrobe in my closet. It hangs behind suits that I no longer wear, partially hidden by a sack of out-of-style clothes awaiting the next drop-off at the Goodwill store. It doesn't look like much now, with its faded colors and threadbare material... but that robe is the only memento I have of my father. And I clearly remember the day in 1943 when it was brand new, and the excitement I felt as a three-year-old child when the mailman delivered it to our house. "*We've* got a new bathrobe," my father announced, "and it's big enough for two!" I knew it was replacing "the old blue one," and I squealed with delight.

On cold mornings, when the air was still crisp, my father would often lift me from my bed, hold me close, and wrap me in the folds of "our" bathrobe. Its faded stripes were a deep maroon back then, and its warm material gave ample protection against a cold morning. We would go into the kitchen and start a fire in the wood-burning stove; my father would break the ice in the wash basin and use its water to prime the kitchen pump, then sit and hold me securely enveloped in that robe as we waited for the breakfast oatmeal to cook and for the "big kids" to get up. I could feel his strong arms around me and hear his soft whispers assuring me that all was well. I could feel the warmth of the crackling fire as it

brought the house to life, while the rising sun welcomed us to another day on the farm.

In the story of the Prodigal Son, neither of the two sons understands the father's relationship with them. Each saw himself more or less as a hired hand – as someone who works for wages. So the youngest son, who has run away, contrives a plan to get his "job" back: "I will arise and go to my father, and I will say to him, 'Father, I have sinned against heaven and before you. I am no longer worthy to be called your son. Treat me as one of your hired servants.'" (Luke 15:18-19) But the father has been waiting, and the minute his son turns homeward, the ring is back on the young man's finger, symbolically reconnecting him to the family that never abandoned him. And in a gesture of belonging, forgiveness, and love, the father's cloak is wrapped around the son's shoulders before he can even finish his apology.

The elder son, too, seems to see himself as a hired hand. "I've stayed with you all these years and worked the farm!" he says. In other words: "You owe me something, because I've been faithful and done the 'right things,' yet you've never even given me a small feast to celebrate." And the father protests, "But son, you are always with me, and everything I have is yours." You have never been *outside* the folds of my robe – we have always been connected; you have always belonged, and every day I give you my love and protection. And you lose nothing by welcoming your brother – so come, let us celebrate, for my other son is home and my robe is big enough for two!

Neither of the two sons understands the unconditional nature of his father's love... any more than *we* understand, despite Jesus' parable, the unconditional love that our Heavenly Father has for *us*.

James R. Welter

I don't wear my father's robe very often; sometimes years pass while it hangs in its assigned place at the back of the closet, next to the Goodwill bag. But I did put it on for each of my two boys when they were about three years old, and held them in its warm embrace. Those were special moments for me, so I always did it when we were alone in the house. I took each of my sons to our old recliner, which they knew as "Daddy's Chair" – "It's big enough for two," I would say – and began to tell the story as I wrapped them in the folds of my father's robe, securing them with its long belt.

They were too young to fully understand, of course, but in telling the story, I felt the warmth of generational connectedness and a sense of my father's presence. I only knew four lines of their favorite song, "Tiny Hand," but I would sing those lines to them over and over again, continuing long after they had fallen asleep in my lap:

"I walk in the rain by your side
I cling to the thumb of your tiny hand
I do everything to help you understand
I love you more than anybody can."

I'm a grandfather now, and that sense of generational connectedness is even more real to me. And time is even more precious. I won't wait for my grandson Calvin's third birthday before I put on my father's robe and take *him* to "Daddy's Chair" to tell the story! And this time, I think I'll sneak a "Grandpa" reference into the song's later verses:

"And I'll sing you the songs of the rainbow
Whisper of the joy that is mine
And I'll do everything to help you understand
I love you more than anybody can."

Holding the child of my child fulfills an ancient scriptural blessing that we received when my wife and I were married thirty-seven years ago: "May you see your children's children..." Now that time has come to pass and the circle is complete – and perhaps I have come to understand what the Prodigal Son did not... and what Jesus' parable is all about.

I hope I have many years left to enjoy the company of our sons and grandson, and I hope there will be other grandchildren. And I hope for one thing more, whenever my time should come: to go home wrapped in the folds of my Father's robe, falling gently asleep as he sings that final refrain...

"I love you more than anybody can!"

INDEX
By Reflection Title

INDEX
By Bible Chapter & Verse

OLD TESTAMENT

NEW TESTAMENT

You may order additional copies of

Come Next Spring

Via our website, **www.AscendingView.com**

OR

Send check or money order for $14.95 per copy,
plus $3.00 shipping and handling
(Indiana residents add 6% sales tax) to:

**Ascending View Publications
231 Crosby Drive
Indianapolis, IN 46227**

Please include your name, address and telephone number
with your order.

Free shipping on orders of more than 10 copies.